Spider in the bush,
Spider on the wall,
Spider with its web,
Most beautiful of all.

How can a creature so small
Know so much?
What a miracle we see
In a spider's geometry!

© TOTEM GRAPHICS

THE WORLD OF SPIDERS

Florida has the honor of having the most diverse group of arachnids (spiders and their relatives) in the eastern US. There are several reasons for this. Because much of Florida lies in subtropical and tropical weather zones, with only occasional freezes, many 'bugs' native to warmer regions are also found in Florida. In addition, the Sunshine State is geographically a crossroads between North America and the Caribbean. "Bugs" have migrated naturally between these areas and have been accidentally transported. Because of its distant past geologic history, the state has arachnids usually found in deserts, such as windscorpions and whipscorpions, and in the tropics, such as whipspiders.

Although not nearly as numerous as their distant relatives, the insects, the arachnids are still a large group. More than 35,000 spider species are known to exist world-wide, but many more have not yet been described. Estimates of how many species of spiders might exist have been as high as 170,000. The most recent estimate is just over 70,000. So at best, only about half the kinds of spiders in the world are presently known. This is probably not good news to those poor souls who suffer from arachnophobia (the fear of spiders).

Only about one in a thousand spiders has venom that is dangerous to humans. Since spiders use venom to subdue prey, it is puzzling why spider venom should be dangerous to people, as we and our nearest relatives are not potential spider prey.

How much of a threat are spiders to humans? There is, of course, some danger, but to put it in perspective, at most seven Florida spider species are potentially dangerous. Bees and wasps kill more people in the US every year than spiders and snakes combined kill in ten years. Dogs and cats kill or seriously injure many more people every year than bees and wasps. Yet it is the poor spider who is the most feared.

Florida is estimated to have about 900 species of spiders. This is more than most states, but fewer than Texas and California. Those two states are not only larger in land area, but they have a greater diversity of habitats, and are connected to further sources of diversity in Mexico. Still, 900 is a lot of spider species.

The average Floridian who pays little more than passing attention to spiders may see as few as 10% (90 spider species) in a lifetime. People who live their lives in a strictly urban environment may see only a third of that small number. Ironically, most of Florida's urban spiders are not even native to Florida, having been imported through commerce. These are the so-called synanthropic (people-loving) spiders, better known as house spiders. Of the roughly 20 species of spiders primarily found in or on human structures, all but two are of certain exotic origin, and the origin of those two is still in question.

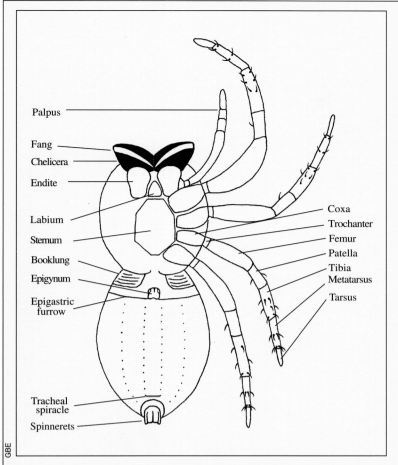

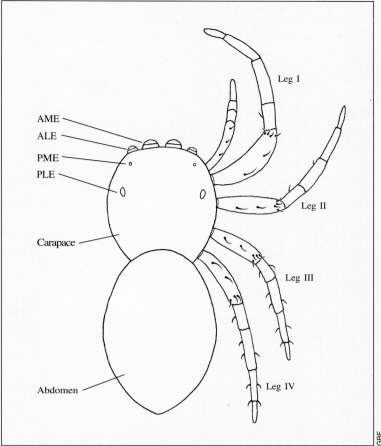

SPIDER ANATOMY

Many spiders are very small in body length. It is easier and more accurate to give their size in millimeters (mm); about 25 mm = one inch. Spiders, like insects, have a hard exoskeleton, a protective shell. Unlike insects (which have three main body parts), spiders only have two main body parts: the cephalothorax (head and thorax fused together) and the abdomen. The cephalothorax is covered on its back by one complete plate, the carapace.

On the carapace are (usually) eight eyes, normally arranged in two side by side rows of four. The eyes closest to the front are the anterior row and consist of two anterior median eyes (AME) and two anterior lateral eyes (ALE). Multiple eyes may be an unusual concept for two-eyed creatures to grasp. It may be helpful to think of median as middle eyes, and lateral as outside eyes. Slightly farther back is the posterior eye row, also consisting of two posterior median eyes (PME) and two posterior lateral eyes (PLE). Sometimes one (or rarely both) of the rows is curved so much that the eyes of that row are not on the same line; in this case that row is considered to have split into two rows, and the spider now has its eyes in three (or four) rows.

The two-segmented jaws (chelicerae) have the last segment on each side formed into a fang.

Spiders also have eight legs, plus a pair of smaller leg-like structures in front called palpi (singular palpus, or palp). Each palp assists with handling food; the basal segment (the endite) helps to manipulate and mash prey. In males, the palps also contain the mating organs. Other structures on the cephalothorax include the labium (sort of the bottom lip) and the sternum (the "chest," roughly equivalent to the same structure on humans).

On the abdomen are the respiratory organs (booklungs and/or tracheae), the spinnerets which spin silk, and the openings to the reproductive tract. A hard plate called the epigynum enclosing the reproductive openings is found on females of most species.

WHAT'S DIFFERENT ABOUT SPIDERS

Spiders are classified as follows. They are placed in the phylum Arthropoda (creatures with exoskeletons and jointed legs), the class Arachnida (arthropods with eight legs and chelicerate jaws), and the order Araneae (spiders). By comparison, the insects are also in the phylum Arthropoda, but in the class Insecta (arthropods with six legs and primitively mandibulate jaws).

There are three main subdivisions of spiders. The Mesothelae are the most primitive group consisting of a few dozen species only found in Southeast Asia, somewhat tarantula-like in appearance but not closely related to tarantulas. The Mygalomorphae are a somewhat larger group consisting of about 2,000 species with a world-wide distribution in temperate and tropical regions, including the tarantulas and their relatives. The Araneomorphae, the rest of the spiders, are sometimes called the "true" spiders. Only members of the Mygalomorphae and Araneomorphae are found in Florida.

How do spiders differ from other arachnids? Two of the most important differences are the presence of spinnerets on the abdomen, and a narrow pedicel (or stalk-like structure) joining the cephalothorax and abdomen. No other arachnid has abdominal spinnerets or a narrow pedicel; instead they have the cephalothorax and abdomen broadly joined together. In the case of harvestmen and mites, all the main body parts are fused together into one unit. Several of the other groups of arachnids also have the palps and/or jaws chelate (with a chela; in other words, like a pincer), which is where the term chelicerae comes from. No spider has a true chela, nor a stinger.

WEBLESS SPIDERS

Many species of Florida spiders do not spin webs, but employ other stategies to catch prey. Most crab spiders and lynx spiders have a gift for choosing sites that are often visited by insects. These spiders wait on flowers or on the topmost shoot of a shrub, like crocodiles at a water hole. The cheetah of the arachnids is the huntsman spider, which specializes in running down fleet-footed cockroaches. The wolf spider, when alerted by the minute vibrations of a beetle's footsteps or by the shadow of a moth flitting across the moonlit sand, springs into explosive action, leaping upon its prey and crushing it with sabre-tooth fangs. At night, sac spiders leave their silken nest and begin questing over leaves and up and down branches where insects rest unsuspecting. Cat-like, jumping spiders stalk their prey, carefully gauging the distance for a lethal pounce. These webless spiders are at least as common and successful as the web weavers. Webless spiders still use silk, but for other purposes.

Wolf Spiders

Family Lycosidae

Wolf spiders are diverse and abundant in most of the world, except the tropics. They have an unusual eye arrangement; their large eyes are located on the sides and back rather than at the front.

Carolina Wolf Spider (above)

This is the largest wolf spider in the US. It makes burrows in sandy habitats, but unlike the burrowing wolf spiders, it does not ambush its prey from the burrow. Rather, it comes out at night and sits on the sand near the burrow, where it can dart back in if threatened by a larger predator. It is gray in color with a double row of white spots on the back of its abdomen, and the underside is all black.

Lycosa carolinensis. **Florida range: northern half. Size: females 22-35 mm, males 18-20 mm. When seen: summer to autumn.**

Field Wolf Spider (left)

One moderately large wolf spider is frequently found in buildings where it is often seen running up and down hallways. It is medium brown with lighter brown markings on the cephalothorax. Although the fangs are big enough to break one's skin, it's bite is little more than a pinprick.

Lycosa lenta. **Florida range: northern half. Size: females 12-18 mm, males 11-17 mm. When seen: spring to summer.**

Top: **the Carolina wolf spider is an imposing creature. Here, the large eyes of its secondary eye row survey for prey as well as potential enemies.**

Left: **this field wolf spider prepares to dart back into its burrow at the approach of a larger animal (in this case, a human).**

Spotted Wolf Spider (above)

This moderately large wolf spider has alternating black and white stripes on the carapace and abdomen, with small black spots on the underside of the pale abdomen. It often hunts in tall grasses, where its striped coloration helps it blend with the foliage.

Rabidosa punctulata. **Florida range: northern half. Size: females 11-17 mm, males 13-15 mm. When seen: summer to autumn.**

Shoreline Wolf Spider (below)

Shoreline wolf spiders have very few hairs on the body and are very pale. The widespread *A. littoralis* is very light tan, blending into the sands along streams and lakes where it is found. The range-restricted *A. sanctaerosae* is white, and is only found on the white sand beaches and islands along the coasts of northwest Florida, Alabama, and Mississippi.

Arctosa littoralis. **Florida range: throughout the state. Size: females and males 11-15 mm. When seen: summer.**
Arctosa sanctaerosae. **Florida range: western Panhandle beaches. Size: adult females 11-15 mm in length, males 9-13 mm. When seen: summer.**

WOLF SPIDER BABIES

Female wolf spiders carry their eggsacs by dragging them behind, attached to the spinnerets. The female must make a strong, papery sac to withstand this abuse; it is so strong that the spiderlings cannot emerge unless the mother spider tears the eggsac open. She does this when she detects her babies moving around inside about a week after they have hatched. After they emerge, the spiderlings ride for several days on their mother's back, hanging onto specialized body hairs; during this time, she protects them from other predators. Within two weeks, they will use up the yolk stored inside their bodies and will leave to begin their own solitary lives.

Nurseryweb Spiders

Family Pisauridae

The common name 'nurseryweb spider' refers to the nest of webbing the female builds for her hatching spiderlings.

The nurseryweb spiders in the genus *Pisaurina* have long, brown bodies with distinctive white striping running their full length. These spiders are most often seen hunting in the long grass of meadows and fields away from water.

Pisaurina mira. **Florida range: northern and central parts of the state. Size: female 12.5-16.5 mm, male 10.5-15.0 mm. When seen: spring to autumn.**

Top: **a female nurseryweb spider feeds on a fly. In a related European species, the male offers a wrapped fly to the female as a courtship gift. While the female feeds, the male mates with her. Since males are in danger of becoming a meal instead of a mate for the female, this is one way in which the male can divert the female's attention to assure his own safety.**

Right: **a view of the nurseryweb which protects the baby spiderlings and gives this group of spiders their common name.**

Far right: **a slender nurseryweb spider (*Pisaurina undulata*) hides on a grass leaf.**

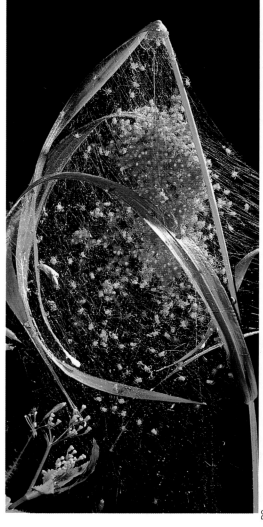

Fishing Spiders

Family Pisauridae (continued)

The fishing spiders in the genus *Dolomedes* are more closely associated with water and some species are very large. Their large size makes it possible for them to capture small fish and amphibians as well as aquatic insects while they sit at the water's edge waiting for something to riffle the surface.

Shoreline Fishing Spider (above)

This dark, greenish-black spider, with white carapace stripes and paired, white spots on the abdomen, is found along the edges of streams and lakes, where it dangles its front legs in the water, attracting prey. Because of the three pairs of spots on the abdomen, this species has sometimes been called the six-spotted fishing spider.

Dolomedes triton. Florida range: statewide. Size: female 15-20 mm, male 13-18 mm. When seen: spring to autumn.

Above: **a juvenile shoreline fishing spider**

Okeefinokee Fishing Spider (left)

This enormous brown spider is often seen on the trunks of cypress trees. Its leg span may reach four inches.

Dolomedes okefinokensis. Florida range: statewide. Size: female 15.0-28.0 mm, male 13.0-28.0 mm. When seen: spring to autumn.

Whitebanded Fishing Spider

This gray spider sometimes has wide, white bands on the sides of the carapace. It can be distinguished by the fact that the head (anterior) region is raised higher than the rest of the carapace. These spiders are found on tree trunks and the outside walls of houses, sometimes well away from water.

Dolomedes albineus. Florida range: statewide. Size: female 15.0-24.0 mm, male 13.0-18.0 mm. When seen: spring to autumn.

BK

Jumping Spiders

Family Salticidae

Jumping spiders belong to the family that has the most species in Florida, with 95 species recorded so far. This is also the largest family of spiders world-wide, with more than 4,400 species described. The family name, Salticidae, is derived from the Latin word meaning "to jump," reflecting the ability of these spiders to accurately jump several times their body length from one point to another.

Jumping spiders come in many shapes and sizes. The largest has a body length of about 25 mm (one inch). The smallest is only about 1.5 mm in length as an adult.

Different species live in all micro-habitats from sub-leaf litter on the ground to the canopy tops of trees. Typically, jumping spiders make nests which are

white, silken bags, where they find some protection from nocturnal predators, molt in order to grow, and lay eggs.

Some species mimic various insects, like ants, beetles, and velvet ants. Others are very cryptic, remaining hidden by blending into tree bark or blades of grass. Some have brilliant colors and unusual decorations of hair tufts and scale-like hairs, especially the males. Often these decorations are displayed during the complex courtship dances males use to entice females to mate.

The most noticeable feature of jumping spiders is their eyes. The anterior median eyes (in front) are by far the largest, with highly developed retinae which give the spider color vision and a high degree of resolution. In addition, the shape of the retina appears to give the spider telephoto vision. These eyes can actually scan by controlling the muscles surrounding the retinal tubes.

Top: **female regal jumper (orange variety).**

Bottom, left: **female regal jumper (gray).**

Bottom, right: **male regal jumper.**

Regal Jumping Spider

The regal jumper is the largest Florida jumping spider and is common throughout the state. Males are black with white markings on the abdomen and legs. Females may be black, gray, tan, brown, or orange, with white or orange abdominal spots. Both sexes have iridescent chelicerae ("jaws") below the eyes, which are green-blue-violet in males, and green or red-violet in females.

Regal jumpers are found in old fields and open woodlands. Adults may inhabit cabbage palms and large saw palmettos. Adult females make their eggsacs under the bark of oaks and pines. Regal jumpers are sometimes found on buildings or fences.

This species is frequently mistaken for the similar Bold Jumping Spider (*Phidippus audax*), more abundant farther north.

Phidippus regius. **Florida range: statewide, especially the peninsular part of the state. Size: females 14-23 mm in length, males 10-18 mm. When seen: adults autumn to spring, but most males die by winter.**

JR

PC

Canopy Jumping Spider

The second largest Florida jumping spider is the canopy jumper. This species resembles the regal jumper, except males have yellow or orange markings instead of white. The females are gray or black with yellow or orange markings. Both sexes have a wide yellow band on each side of the "head" region, which is almost always lacking in the regal jumper. The color of the chelicerae is orange-yellow-green in both sexes.

Canopy jumpers are most often found in moist woodlands, usually in trees; they may be found on man-made structures as well. Females make their eggsacs under the dead bark of oak and pines, especially those that have been struck by lightning.

Phidippus otiosus. **Florida range: north of Lake Okeechobee. Size: females 12-18 mm, males 8-12 mm. When seen: adult females autumn to spring, males in autumn only.**

THE EYES OF JUMPING SPIDERS

The retinal cell density of jumping spider anterior median eyes is in the same order of magnitude as human eyes. For an animal five orders of magnitude smaller than a human, this gives incredible resolution. Jumping spiders are considered to have the best eyes of any "bug." Perhaps the old saying, "eyes like an eagle," should be changed to "eyes like a jumping spider."

Jumping spiders have other eyes with less complex retinae which probably serve mostly as motion detectors. The field of view of the anterior lateral eyes overlaps in front, and gives the spider binocular vision, *considerably aiding its ability to jump accurately. The posterior median eyes are small, with no known function, although it is suspected they may detect movement from above. The posterior lateral eyes have a very wide angle of vision that, when combined with the other eyes, gives the spider a 320 degree range.*

Large jumping spiders can typically see motion of larger animals up to four meters or more away. Insects and other smaller organisms are usually detected at less than one meter.

When stalking prey, the spider visually *assesses the intended victim. It appears to be able to evaluate the escape potential of the prey and to adjust its own capture behavior accordingly. For example, a caterpillar may walk slowly, and the spider can take its time to circle around to the front, then lunge and bite the caterpillar behind the head. On the other hand, when stalking a fly, the spider will be very stealthy, creep directly toward the fly, and take a long leap, biting the fly at the base of the wings. All things considered, the prey capture behavior of jumping spiders is remarkably similar to that of cats.*

Red Beauty Jumping Spider

Another pretty jumping spider is the red beauty. Its species name, *pulcherrimus*, means "most beautiful" in Latin. It has white bands behind the posterior eyes, and red on top of the abdomen with white spots on a black median stripe. Females make their eggsacs in rolled leaves.

Phidippus pulcherrimus. **Florida range: statewide, usually in moist understory and shrubs in older fields. Size: females 8-11 mm, males 7-9 mm. When seen: spring.**

Pantropical Jumping Spider

(right and far right)

The pantropical jumper is a widespread, introduced tropical species, usually found on man-made structures, and occasionally in agricultural areas, like citrus groves. It is fairly robust, but not as large as the *Phidippus* jumpers. Females are brown with tan markings. Males are striped lengthwise black and white, with the stripes continuing onto the face.

Plexippus paykulli. **Florida range: statewide. Size: adult females 9-12 mm in length, males 8-10 mm. When seen: all year, but more prevalent in summer and fall.**

Top: a red beauty jumper. This specimen is a female which is full of eggs (gravid).

Left, and below: two views of the pantropical jumper. Both are males (indicated by the lengthwise stripes which continue across the face). The eyes of this species seem unusually expressive, thanks to a ringlight photo flash.

PROBLEM SOLVING SPIDERS

Jumping spiders are problem solvers! Imagine you are walking along a wide river and you feel hungry. You see an island out in the river with some berry bushes, but you cannot get there directly because the current is too strong. You see that a tree has fallen from the opposite bank to the island, and then you notice that there is a rope bridge downstream where you could cross to the other bank. By crossing the bridge and then traversing the tree trunk, *you could get to the berry bushes. This simple example is just like the real life problems that jumping spiders encounter every day. They see a target (whether a prey item or a potential mate), and they must figure out how to get to it, even if by a circuitous route. Sometimes they must go where they are out of sight of the target, or even go away from it initially. Fortunately, they can remember locations in three-dimensional space, so they end up where they intended.*

Red Velvet Jumper (Apache)

This attractive spider is infrequently seen in Florida. It is black with bright red scales on top of the head and abdomen. The chelicerae are bright iridescent green. These spiders only occur in xeric (dry) fields. They appear to mimic large wingless wasps, variously known as velvet ants, cow killers, or mutillids, which have a powerful sting. Males actually imitate the jerky walk of these wasps. Females with eggsacs have been found under bark on oak logs.

Phidippus apacheanus. **Florida range: statewide, but especially in sandhill habitats. Size: females 10-15 mm, males 7-12 mm. When seen: adults in autumn, females rarely to spring.**

PC

PC

Gray Wall Jumping Spider

The gray wall jumper is an introduced species commonly seen on buildings and bridges. It is rather flattened in appearance. Females are mostly gray, with a yellow transverse band across the face. Males are striped black and white, with a black face.

Menemerus bivittatus. **Florida range: statewide. Size: adult females are 8-10 mm in length, males 7-9 mm. When seen: all year, but more prevalent in spring and summer.**

Twinflagged Jumping Spider

This mottled brown and black jumping spider would be fairly inconspicuous if not for the bright silvery white spots on each palp (the leg-like structures on either side of the face). The constant bobbing of these palps moves the white spots and draws attention to these little spiders which frequently appear in homes. Normally, these spiders live on leaf litter and tree trunks in moist woodlands. They have been seen eating ants and mosquitoes.

Anasaitis canosa. **Florida range: statewide. Adults: females 5-6 mm, males 4-5 mm. When seen: all year, but less frequently in winter.**

GBE

PC

Ground Jumping Spiders

A number of ground-dwelling, jumping spiders have males with amazing leg and face decorations. Females are usually gray or brown in color. Many of these are in the genus *Habronattus*, the largest genus in North America with more than 95 species. There are at least eleven species in Florida. Females are usually 5-7 mm in length, males 4-6 mm.

Ocala Ground Jumper (top)

In this species, the male has a bright red band below the eyes, and the body is black and brown. The third pair of legs have a fancy spine that projects from the "knee" that is displayed during courtship. The female is mostly light brown. It is found in dry fields of central Florida scrub.

Habronattus ocala. Florida range: central peninsula. Size: females 4.7-5.9 mm, males 3.9-4.0 mm. When seen: summer.

GBE

WHAT IS AN ARACHNID?

The vast array of animals with external skeletons and jointed legs is known to biologists as the arthropods. The great majority belong to three big sub-groups. First is the Crustacea, such as lobsters, crabs, and pillbugs, most of which are aquatic, with gills and at least five pairs of legs. Second are the Insecta, which have only three pairs of legs, and often have wings. Third, are the Arachnida, which usually have four pairs of legs and another set of appendages in front modified as predatory organs, or sensory feelers, or (in male spiders) as sex organs. The general impression given by arachnids is that they are compact (the body is divided into only one or two sections) with a lot of legs. This book concentrates on the most familiar group of arachnids, the spiders, but there is also a short section at the end dealing with the other Florida arachnids.

Eyebrowed Ground Jumper

(above)

Males of this species have bright green front legs and cute white "eyebrow" markings over the front eyes. Females are light brown. The eyebrowed ground jumper occurs in sandhill communities in the interior of the peninsula.

Habronattus notialis. Florida range: northern half of state. Size: both sexes 4.5-6.0 mm. When seen: summer.

Pike's Slender Jumping Spider

Pike's slender jumper has an unusually long shape for a jumping spider. The female is grayish yellow, while the male is black with white transverse markings. Both sexes hold their legs lengthwise, enhancing their stretched appearance. The female easily blends into dying grass blades and stems. The male's pattern may help break up its outline so it won't be conspicuous. These spiders are found in fields, marshes, and along the edges of bodies of water.

Marpissa pikei. **Florida range: statewide. Size: adults of both sexes 7-9 mm in length. When seen: spring to summer.**

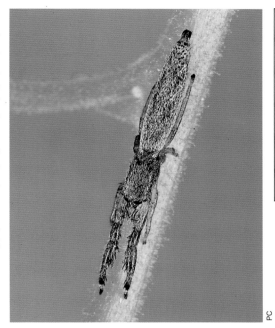

Above: **female dimorphic jumper.**

Above: **male dimorphic jumper**

Dimorphic Jumping Spider

This species of jumping spider has two kinds of male coloration. One type is mottled with gray and red like the female, whereas the other is black with white legs. Amazingly, the black male has three large black tufts of hair on top of its head. The different color forms correspond to differences in the courtship each type of male displays. Black males court females from farther away and stand very tall, whereas the other males court at closer range and hold themselves very low. Apparently, the females don't prefer one over the other. This species is common in moist woodland understory.

Maevia inclemens. **Florida range: northern half of state. Size: adult females 8-9 mm in length, males 7-8 mm. When seen: spring to early summer.**

Bronze Lake Jumper *(above)*

This species is abundant in the tall, thick grass which borders the edges of lakes.

Eris flava. **Florida range: statewide. Size: female mm, male mm. When seen: spring to fall.**

A NOISELESS PATIENT SPIDER

A noiseless patient spider,
I mark'd where on a little promontory
it stood isolated,
Mark'd how to explore the vacant vast
surrounding,
It launched forth filament, filament,
filament, out of itself,
Ever unreeling them, ever tirelessly
speeding them.

And you, O my soul where you stand,
Surrounded, detached, in measureless
oceans of space,
Ceaselessly musing, venturing, throwing,
seeking the spheres to connect them,
Till the bridge you will need be form'd,
till the ductile anchor hold,
Till the gossamer thread you fling
catch somewhere, O my soul.

-Walt Whitman

Magnolia Green Jumping Spider

This bizarre spider hardly looks like a jumper. The legs and palps as well as the male jaws are all rather long. Both sexes are a pale, translucent green, with white and red scales on top of the head. The black retinae of the eyes can be seen through the clear outer lens. This spider lives in all types of woodlands, often on broad-leaved evergreens, such as magnolia and live oak.

Lyssomanes viridis. **Florida range: statewide. Adults: females 7-8 mm in length, males 6-8 mm. When seen: spring to early summer.**

Right: the awesome face of a male magnolia green jumping spider. The spectacular front eyes sometimes appear to rotate in their sockets. The retinae of these large eyes are controlled by six pairs of muscles. These muscles can make the eyes move in any direction. Sometimes the eyes move independently, much like a chameleon. Since the retinae appear black in color, they can be seen easily in translucent spiders such as this one. A person can tell if he is being watched by a spider. If you can see the black retinae, the eyes are aimed directly at you.

Below: a *Lyssomanes* female on a black-eyed Susan flower, waiting for prey. Composite flowers such as this one are not the normal habitat for a Lyssomanes spider.

JUMPING SPIDER COURTSHIP

Courtship is a potentially hazardous event for most spiders, and different kinds of spiders have developed their own methods for dealing with it. Jumping spiders, with their outstanding eyesight, have evolved a complex, visually-oriented courtship, that consists of displays of ornaments and/or patterns of movement. The ornaments are hair tufts and fringes on the "face" and legs, prominent on males, but less pronounced or absent on females. The visual courtship is performed by a male who finds a female outside of her nest. Some species have, in addition, special organs which produce vibrations and even sound, which is used to enhance the visual display. Studies of a few species have even found a totally different vibratory courtship a male uses when he finds a female inside her nest. Considering both the capture of prey and courtship, jumping spiders have as complex a set of behaviors as any vertebrate that has been studied (with the exception of humans).

Woodland Jumper (top)

In this large, slender species, the male (top, right) and female (top, left) have a very different appearance. This species is common in woodland understory and on shrubs in fields.

Thiodina sylvana. **Florida range: statewide in many habitats. Size: females 8-10 mm, males 7-9 mm. When seen: adults mostly spring to autumn.**

Workman Jumper (right)

The workman jumper looks like a smaller version of the regal jumping spider. Workman jumpers are found in dry, sandy fields, where they live on small scrub oaks and on other small, woody plants.

Phidippus workmani. **Florida range: statewide in scrub and sandhill habitats. Size: females 8-11mm, males 7-10mm. When seen: Adults in mid-summer.**

Antmimic Jumping Spider

The largest ant mimics among the jumping spiders live on the ground and low shrubs. They are brown with white markings which imitate indentations. Males have long chelicerae which imitate an ant carrying a parcel. These spiders appear to mimic large ponerine ants (a primitive type of ant) which have a potent sting.

Sarinda hentzi. **Florida range: statewide. Size: Adult females 6-8 mm in length, males 5-6 mm. When seen: spring to summer.**

SPIDERS WHICH MIMIC ANTS

It is easy to tell antmimic spiders from real ants. The real ants have antennae extending from the front of their heads and their abdomens are clearly divided into segments.

Mimicry is a situation in which one organism (the mimic) looks like another (the model) to gain protection. Ants are a common model because they are aggressive, can sting or bite, and have relatively few enemies. Many other organisms have evolved to look like ants to gain protection from their own enemies.

Spiders which mimic ants wave one of their front pairs of legs around like antennae to enhance their overall resemblance to ants. Oddly, different species don't necessarily use the same pair of legs for this purpose. Some species use the first pair and others the second pair.

PC

Hentzia Jumping Spiders

Spiders of the genus *Hentzia* are unusual in that the males of most species have their chelicerae (jaws) elongated, flattened, and extended forward. This is the only genus of spiders in Florida whose jaws are of this shape.

Hentzia grenada. Florida range: peninsula. Size: female 4.1-5.5 mm, male 4.0-5.7 mm. When seen: spring to fall.
Hentzia mitrata: Florida range: statewide. Size: female 2.9-4.5, male 3.5-4.1 mm. When seen: spring to fall.
Hentzia palmarum: Florida range: statewide. Size: female 4.7-6.1 mm, male 4.0-5.3 mm. When seen spring to fall.

PC

NICHOLAS HENTZ: AMERICA'S FIRST ARACHNOLOGIST

Hentz was the first American to seriously study spiders, beginning with a scientific paper in 1821. He named and described many species of spiders. He was also a very eccentric individual who, while talking to a friend, might suddenly fall to his knees for a brief prayer before continuing the conversation. He was a skilled painter and teacher of French who earned his living as headmaster at a number of girls' schools, since the spider trade in those days paid very little.

Top: a striped Hentz jumper *(Hentzia grenada),* a common Florida jumper with unusual forward-directed jaws. This species is found on cycads and small palms.

Above: a male pale Hentz jumper *(Hentzia mitrata),* shown here eating a fly. This photo was taken at Myakka River State Park. Notice that this species does not have long jaws.

Left: a male common Hentz jumper *(Hentzia palmarum).* This species is distinctive because its jaws are very long and extend a considerable distance toward the front, sometimes as long as the carapace. This species occurs in a variety of understory and field habitats, and may be abundant on mangroves.

PC

Sac Spiders

Family Clubionidae

There have been scattered reports of the bites of other Florida spiders causing small necrotic spots. The most frequently reported have been those of certain kinds of sac spiders.

These small, yellow spiders often get into homes, especially in winter. Sac spiders are named for their habit of resting inside a silken nest hidden in a rolled leaf. Here they molt and lay eggs. They are active at night and can run swiftly. They are frequently found in native fields and agricultural areas.

Cheiracanthium inclusum. Florida range: statewide. Size: adults of both sexes 5-7 mm in length. When seen: all year, especially summer.

Top: a sac spider resting in its silk sack.

A LOT OF SPIDERS

Early one morning in late September, as a coffee-toting commuter steps out to his car, he sees that the first mists of fall have advertised the snares of spiders. Across the little flyways between branches are stretched radial nets and artful tangles. In layers from shrub-top to the ground are the small, lethal trampolines set for carelessly leaping leafhoppers. Silk-lined tunnels lead from the dark interiors of weed clumps out onto the delicate silk carpet spread to catch the tiny claws of pedestrian ants. Droplet hung strands loosely loop from twig to twig, marking the passage of hunting spiders creeping about to catch sleeping flies. "Man!" says the commuter, "There's a lot of spiders!" He's right. There are a lot of spiders. Exactly how many spiders can make their homes on an acre of Florida landscape depends on the richness of the habitat. Along the edges of lakes and marshes, the periodic waves of midges and mayflies that fly over shoreline shrubs support huge numbers of spiders, often hundreds in a single large shrub. A random handful of leaf litter grabbed from a diverse north Florida forest almost always includes spiders, often many. Less luxuriant habitats, such as dry Florida scrub, have fewer spiders, but even for such habitats, an estimate of 10,000 spiders per acre would probably be reasonable. Nobody knows for sure because spider counting has rarely been attempted in Florida. Any such project is likely to produce surprising results.

SPIDER FOLKLORE

Spiders seldom wear white hats in European cultures. This bias is typified by the giant, evil spiders in J. R. R. Tokein's Middle Earth saga, a masterpiece brilliantly assembled from all the most enduring stereotypes of European folklore. Charlotte's Web is definitely battling against powerful currents in Anglo-American culture. In other cultures, however, spiders are often viewed more favorably, even though the dangers of venomous species, especially the various widow spiders, are well recognized.

Spiders are often admired for their spinning and weaving and in numerous myths a spider god or goddess is credited with teaching humans to make textiles. A good example can be found in the Navajo Tribe which is known for its fine woven products. Navajos believe that their goddess, Spider Woman, taught the tribe's ancestors to weave in the style of the open-hub web design shown on page 30 of this book. To this day, Navajo weavings always follow this design. The hole may be small and hard to find in modern Navajo textile designs, but it is always included. The almost invisible filaments that spiders use to move from place to place are the basis of another series of American Indian myths in which prisoners escape from an unclimbable butte, or people ascend up into the sky, or people and animals climb down from the sky. Spiders are involved in the creation stories and tales of the search for fire. Spider gods and demigods also appear in stories as tricksters in both African and American Indian cultures in which humor plays a larger role than in most mainstream religions.

PC

Crab Spiders

Family Thomisidae

Crab spiders can be easily identified because their first two pairs of legs are much longer than the last two pairs. This is one of the larger families of spiders, with over 2,000 species described world-wide.

Flower Crab Spider (top)

The flower crab spider is similar to the whitebanded crab spider, but is smaller and lacks the facial ridge. Numerous small dark hairs are noticeable on the body. Females and males are similar in color, usually white, less often yellow, and occasionally with red blotches on the abdomen. Males are much smaller than females. Both sexes under magnification are noticeably hairy. Flower crab spiders occur in similar types of flowers as the whitebanded crab spider.

Misumenops celer. Florida range: statewide. Size: adult females 5-6 mm in length, males 3-4 mm. When seen: spring to summer.

PC

Top: a flower crab spider waiting for prey on a gaillardia flower.

Left: a twig crab spider on a leaf, extending its legs as it normally would do along a twig where it would be much less conspicuous.

Opposite page, top left: a whitebanded crab spider on a zinnia flower. The female can change from white to yellow for camouflage.

Opposite page, center: a whitebanded crab spider awaits prey on a composite flower.

Twig Crab Spider (left)

Twig crab spiders are unusual because the face slants downward and forward. They are dark gray or brown with inconspicuous reddish brown markings. They hold their legs extended front and back along a twig, and essentially look like a small knot. They ambush insects which walk along or land on the twig. Males are only slightly smaller than females. Dry oak woodlands are a favorite habitat.

Tmarus rubrocinctus. Florida range: statewide. Size: adult females 7-8 mm in length, males 6-7 mm. When seen: late spring to summer.

BALLOONING

The young flower crab spider in the photo above is preparing to balloon. Many newborn spiderlings begin their careers with this dangerous aerial adventure. Soon after emerging from the eggsac, they climb up a tall grass blade or twig, face into the wind, and release silk filaments. As the filaments reach a length of one or two yards, they pull the baby spider from its perch. Ballooning is the most important means of dispersal for many spiders. Once airborne like a kite that has gotten away from its owner, the spider has little control over its fate. One spider may land at the edge of a pond where a supply of midges awaits its first small web. The next spider may land two feet beyond in water patrolled by hungry minnows. Why take such a risk? One reason: a site would be excessively crowded with potentially cannibalistic siblings if all stayed at home.

Also, the mother's habitat may not be ideal for the babies since the mother is feeding on much larger prey. But the spiders do not usually land at random. They are transported by the same air currents and encounter the same obstacles, so they tend to cluster a bit in landing areas. Also dropping by will be wind-borne insects such as aphids and thrips and wind-borne pollen, all of which provide an excellent source of food for the young spiders.

When weather conditions are just right, thousands of spiders may balloon at the same time. When they come down, they may cover the landscape with fine strands of silk, which may be very conspicuous. This is known as gossamer. A warm spell during autumn may induce this mass ballooning event. The drapery of silk gave rise to the expression "gossamer summer."

Whitebanded Crab Spider

The whitebanded crab spider has a white ridge on its face below the eyes. A female may be white or yellow (sometimes with red or black spots), and can change from one color to another, depending on what color flower it is sitting in. This ability helps protect the spider from predators.

The whitebanded crab spider attacks insects attracted to the nectar and pollen of flowers. Composite plants (like asters) and goldenrod are among the kinds of flowers which host these spiders.

Males are dark brown and much smaller than females. Both sexes seem to be mostly devoid of hairs on the body.

Misumenoides formosipes. Florida range: statewide. Size: adult females 8-10 mm in length, males 4-5 mm. When seen: late summer to autumn.

Lynx Spiders

Family Oxyopidae

Lynx spiders form a small, world-wide family with a very unusual eye arrangement. Two small eyes are in front, followed by six eyes in a hexagonal pattern. Most species are hunters, although one small tropical group makes a small sheet web.

Green Lynx Spider

The green lynx spider is the largest of its family. True to its name, it is mostly green, with some white spotting. But if the plant it is on has reddish or purplish foliage or flowers, the spider is able to suffuse these colors into its abdomen to increase its ability to blend into its background. It leaps onto insects, enclosing them in a basket made by its spiny legs.

Peucetia viridans. **Florida range: statewide. Size: adult females 12-15 mm in length, males 10-13 mm. When seen: late summer to autumn.**

Top: a female green lynx prepares to pounce on another predator, a damselfly.
Center: the face of a green lynx shows the unusual eye arrangement.
Bottom, left: a mother green lynx stands guard over her recently hatched young. She spits venom at intruders.
Bottom, right: green lynx typically ambush prey by waiting near the tops of plants.

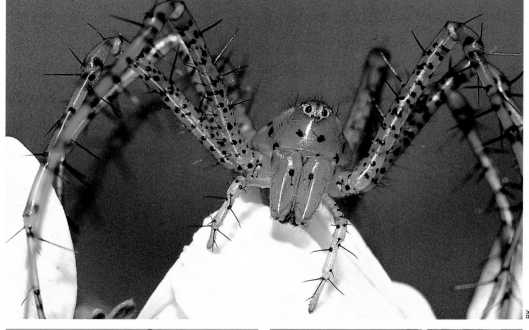

Striped Lynx Spider (top)

This smaller version of the green lynx is yellow with four dark stripes on the head region. Males have a black abdomen that is sometimes iridescent. It is a field dweller, usually found on grasses and small shrubs.

Oxyopes salticus. Florida range: statewide. Size: adult females 5-6 mm in length, males 4-5 mm. When seen: late spring to summer.

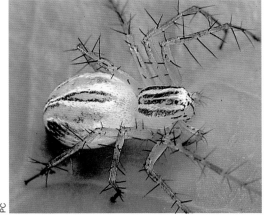

Top: a female striped lynx spider has stripes on its face as well as on the top of its carapace.

Above left: a female striped lynx.

Above, right: a male striped lynx. Note the beautiful iridescent color of the abdomen.

Bark Lynx Spider (left)

The bark lynx spider, like the twig crab spider, is gray and looks like a knot on a twig. Extensive leg fringes help this spider blend its outline with tree bark, usually that of oak trees. It is mostly active at night.

Hamataliwa grisea. Florida range: statewide. Size: adult females 6-7 mm in length, males 5-6 mm. When seen: late spring to summer.

21

PC

INTRODUCTION TO HOUSEHOLD SPIDERS

It is a tribute to the adaptability of our own species that we humans are able to thrive in conditions found in the normal Florida household. The conditions are strikingly different from most natural habitats. Many animals are exquisitely sensitive to day length. In Florida homes the number of hours of light and dark vary wildly. Many animals schedule their lives around temperature or are activated by changes in temperature. Most homes lack these stimuli. More importantly, few animals are adapted to the perpetual dryness of the modern Florida home. Although many spiders wander in from outdoors, almost all of these are doomed from the moment that they scamper over the threshold. True household spiders, those that can survive indoors generation after generation, are a small, select group. Their origins tend to be caves and dry, rocky overhangs in tropical and subtropical lands. Even these species often show a decided preference for the bathroom or the area around the kitchen sink. The prey of these spiders include household insects (an equally select group) and the various insects that get trapped in houses, usually those lured in by lights at night. Basements (rare in Florida) and garages are more hospitable to spiders, primarily because of higher humidity, but garages may suffer from the problem of excessive heat in the summer. In contrast, the outside surfaces of a Florida

Ghost Spiders

Family Anyphaenidae

Ghost spiders are similar in appearance to sac spiders, and used to be placed in the same family. They differ in that they have two rows of club-shaped hairs on the bottoms of their feet, and their tracheal spiracle is located well in front of the spinnerets, unlike most spiders which have their tracheal opening right in front of the spinnerets.

Yellow Ghost Spider (top)

This ghost spider resembles the sac spider, but it is slightly larger. It also gets in houses, where it hunts insects and smaller spiders. It has been reported to feed on leaf miners, no small trick as these pests are actually inside the layers of a leaf!

Hibana velox. **Florida range: statewide. Size: adults of both sexes 7-9 mm in length. When seen: all year, especially summer.**

Top: a yellow ghost spider with eggs.

Right: green ghost spider.

home are likely to have a rich selection of spiders, including all the indoor species and a batch of species found in natural habitats. As one moves away from the house into the ornamental plantings or more natural habitats, most of the household spiders disappear, replaced by less specialized species.

PC

Green Ghost Spider (above)

Although its scientific name means white (the color it turns after it is preserved in alcohol), this small, common spider is actually pale green. It runs around on foliage at night, hunting its prey.

Wulfila alba. **Florida range: statewide. Size: adults of both sexes about 4 mm in length. When seen: spring.**

Giant Crab Spiders

(Huntsman, Housekeeping Spider, "Banana" Spider)

Family Sparassidae

This giant crab spider, usually known as the huntsman or housekeeping spider, is the largest spider a Florida homeowner is likely to encounter in the house. It is an introduced species, originally from Asia. The females may have a leg span of 10 cm (4 inches), and males, although they have smaller bodies, may have a legspan of 12.5 cm (5 inches).

While these spiders typically are found indoors, they are found outdoors as well in South Florida. They are nocturnal predators which feed on cockroaches, silverfish, and other insects. They often are seen on walls or ceilings. They are very fast runners and can sometimes be heard scuttling across floors.

Although not dangerously venomous to humans, these large spiders can give a bite that will swell considerably, with a large purple blotch in the center. The swelling may take several days to subside.

Heteropoda venatoria. **Florida range: throughout peninsular Florida, but more common in the southern half. Size: adult females 20-30 mm in length, males 15-25 mm. When seen: throughout the year.**

Center: **a mother housekeeping spider carrying her disc-shaped eggsac.**

Crevice Spiders

Family Filistatidae

Crevice spiders are a small group found world-wide. Only one species is found in Florida.

Southern Crevice Spider

The southern crevice spider, also known as the southern house spider, is abundant, especially on older, wooden buildings. It makes a flat, sheet-like web that consists of fine, woolly silk (cribellate silk) that entangles insects. The web has a hole in the middle leading to a crevice where the spider hides, waiting for prey to become trapped. The remains of prey and other debris accumulate in the web making this one of the worst household "cobwebs."

The two sexes are very different in appearance. Females are robust and dark charcoal-gray without any markings, whereas males are slender and light tan in color, with a brown streak on the head region. Males are frequently mistaken for brown recluse spiders, but crevice spiders have longer appendages and eight eyes clumped together.

A few cases of bites from this species are known which caused pain and moderate swelling lasting a couple of days. Like the brown recluse, the fangs are tiny and the spider must be pressed against the skin in order for it to effectively bite.

Kukulcania hibernalis. **Florida range: statewide. Size: Adult females 12-15 mm in length, males 10-12 mm, but the long legs make the males seem much larger. When seen: females all year (females may live for several years), males in spring to summer.**

SPIDERS IN THE BIBLE

*There be four things which
are little upon the earth,
But they are exceeding wise;
The ants are a people not strong,
Yet they prepare their
meat in the summer;
The conies are but a feeble folk,
yet they make their houses in the rocks;
The locusts have no king,
yet go they forth all of them by bands;
The spider taketh hold with her hands,
And is in Kings' palaces.*

Proverbs 30: 24-28

Wandering Spiders

Family Ctenidae

There are some notorious members of this family in South America, large and fearsome spiders which have caused human deaths. It would not be too surprising to find that a Florida wandering spider can also give a serious bite.

Florida Wandering Spider

The Florida wandering spider is very similar in size and shape to a medium-sized wolf spider. It is dark brown with a broad pale stripe extending down the full body length. On the abdomen, the stripe is partially broken into chevron markings.

This spider is particularly prevalent in moist, wooded areas. It may also be around the mouths of caverns, and is an excellent climber. Numerous records of this spider have come from homes built in wooded environments. The species is found throughout peninsular Florida.

One suspected bite from this species occurred in Ft. Myers to a woman who subsequently had a necrotic wound, as well as prolonged effects to her nervous system, such as disorientation. This may, in fact, be the culprit responsible for repeated diagnoses of brown recluse bite in Florida.

Ctenus captiosus. **Florida range: throughout peninsula. Size: adult females 12-16 mm in length, males 9-13 mm. When seen: adults in spring to summer, but large sub-adults may be seen in autumn and winter.**

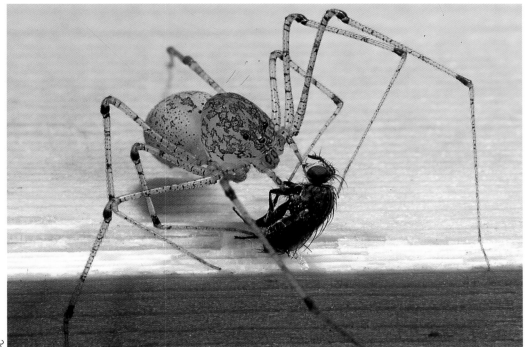

PC

Spitting Spiders

Family Scytodidae

Spitting spiders are another small group found world-wide. They are closely related to recluse spiders, although their venom is not toxic to humans. They also have six eyes in three pairs. Their most conspicuous feature is a high, domed carapace (the top part of the cephalothorax, the combined "head" and "thorax"). Beneath it are large modified salivary glands in which glue is produced.

Above: **a spitting spider sticking down a fly by spitting glue.**

Like the recluse spiders, spitting spiders stealthily approach their prey until within range. They have taken safety one step further by not initially contacting the prey at all. Instead, they spit glue on their prey that holds it down while the spider leisurely saunters over to inject venom to subdue it, then eats it. Some species build an irregular web to help impede prey and give the spider more time to approach.

Some species of spitting spiders are semi-social. One large species with long legs is found in and on houses where it sometimes lives in extended family groups in a dense web. In homes where it is found, other spiders are usually scarce because spitting spiders can be deadly to other species.

Spitting spiders are all very similar, differing noticeably only in their color patterns, sizes, and the lengths of their extremely slender legs. Most species have a mottled color pattern that makes them hard to see in their natural environment. However, when in houses, this pattern can make them obvious, even though some species seem to prefer living in houses.

One species is mostly reddish brown in color, but it is usually found outdoors. There are at least five species of spitting spiders found in Florida.

Scytodes sp. **Florida range: central peninsula in buildings, likely introduced. Size: adult females 9-10 mm in length, males 8-9 mm. When seen: all year.**

Scytodes thoracica. **Florida range: northern half in buildings. Size: Adults 5-6 mm in length. When seen: all year.**

Scytodes fusca. **Reddish brown, common on palm trunks and under the bark of other trees. Florida range: southern half of state. Size: adults 5-6 mm in length. When seen: all year.**

Longlegged Spiders, Cellar Spiders

Family Pholcidae

The common name, cellar spider, comes from the fact that a few introduced species are common in cellars in cool climates. These spiders have extremely long legs compared to their body size, often ten times or more the body length. Otherwise, these are relatively small spiders, 8 mm or less in length. They are superficially similar to the daddy-long-legs, another group of arachnids (harvestmen, order Opiliones). They are not known to be venomous to humans.

These spiders have an interesting defensive behavior called "bouncing." When disturbed, the spider will begin oscillating up and down in its tangled web so quickly that it becomes a blur, making it very difficult for a potential predator to attack. Some orbweaving spiders use a similar defensive action. If the web is actually invaded, the spider can run off the web at a remarkably fast speed, then it will find a concealed spot to hide.

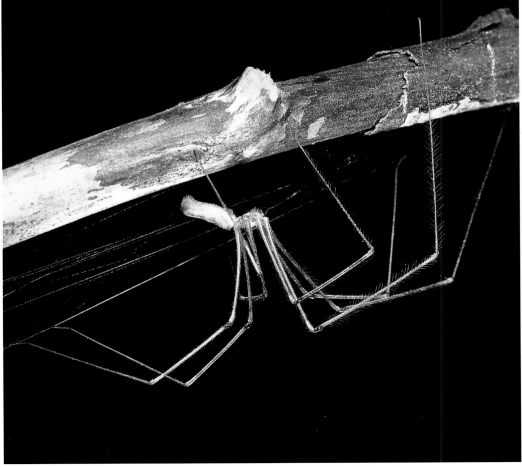

DL

Cobweb Weavers

Family Theridiidae

This large family consists mostly of small spiders which make three-dimensional tangle webs. It includes the infamous widow spiders. Widows are well known to almost everyone. There are four Florida species; two occur on buildings. Widow spiders make a tangle web with a characteristic dense conical area in an upper corner where the spider hides.

Southern Black Widow

The southern black widow is found in most Florida habitats. It is shiny, jet black with a red, hourglass-shaped mark on the underside of the abdomen (which is about the size of a large pea), and another red spot just above the spinnerets (the silk-producing appendages). The legs are long, slender, and entirely black. The eggsacs are pear-shaped, white, and smooth.

It prefers dark, damp, protected web sites close to the ground. Typical places to find it are in hollows under logs, under low shrubs, in water meter holes, in empty nursery cans, and in outbuildings like barns, sheds, and garages. When outhouses were in common use, black widows were frequently found in them.

Latrodectus mactans. **Florida range: statewide. Size: adult females 8-12 mm, males 4-6 mm. When seen: females most of year, although they tend to die out in the autumn; males in spring.**

PC

PC

Top: female southern black widow pulling silk from her spinnerets.

Left: black widow eaten by a preying mantis.

Above: a male black widow.

Opposite, top: black widow eggsac opened to reveal eggs and young spiders hatching.

Opposite page, lower left: a northern black widow. Note the red spots on the back.

Opposite page, lower right: a brown widow with her characteristic tufted eggsacs.

DL

A FLORIDA SPIDER STORY

Some years ago, an enthusiastic Florida teacher brought a black widow spider into an elementary school classroom as an example of a cool animal with interesting adaptations. The spider had an eggsac, which in due course hatched and the tiny spiders escaped through little holes in the cage. The students immediately began to manifest an alarming series of reactions, including flu-like symptoms, skin irritations, pimples and unexplained agitation and hyper-sensitivity among children who thought they might have been bitten by deadly spiders. The teacher was sent home in disgrace, and the school was fumigated. All the consternation could have been avoided by realizing that the jaws of a newborn black widow are too weak to puncture the skin of a child and that the amount of venom that affects humans does not occur in baby black widows.

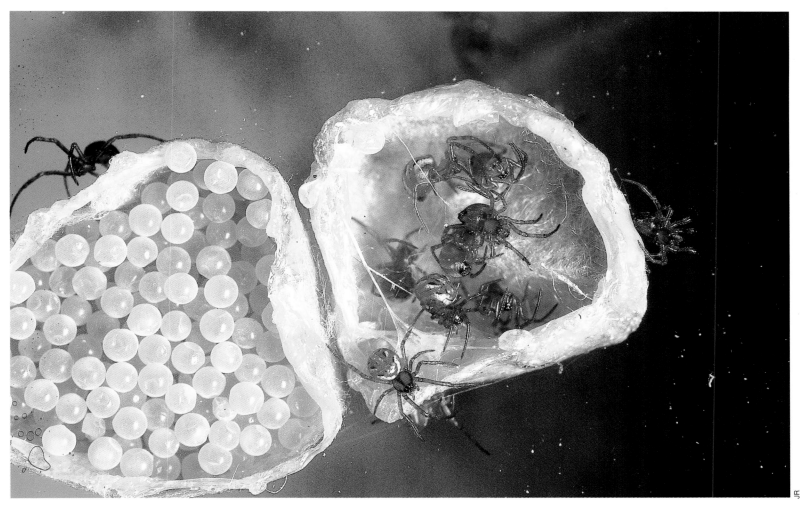

Northern Black Widow

The northern black widow is very similar to the southern black widow, except it has a row of red spots down the middle of its back (top of the abdomen), and the hourglass mark is broken in the middle. It makes its tangled web on the ends of tree branches.

Latrodectus variolus. **Florida range: Panhandle. Size and when seen: similar to southern black widow.**

Brown Widow Spider

The brown widow is an introduced species originally from Africa but now found in tropical and subtropical areas world-wide. Its range is expanding in Florida. Compared to the black widow, it is very light to very dark brown, and the hourglass mark is orange instead of red. The legs are banded with dark brown and a lighter color alternately on each segment. The back of the abdomen may have paired light-colored slash marks, as well as a central row of pale spots. These markings may be absent on darker specimens.

These spiders are abundant on buildings of all types and can be found under the eaves, on windows and drain pipes, and under benches. Undersides of mobile homes may provide web sites for dozens of brown widows. Fortunately, these are very timid spiders, but bites do occur occasionally.

Latrodectus geometricus. **Florida range: throughout most of peninsula and spreading northward. Size: adult females 7-10 mm, males 2 mm. When seen: similar to southern black widow.**

Red Widow Spider

This gorgeous spider is only found in the sand pine scrub habitats of central and southern Florida. It gets its name from the red-orange color of its cephalothorax and appendages. Its abdomen is black with a row of red dots like the northern black widow, but these are encircled with yellow. The hourglass mark is reduced to a single flat triangle. Usually the web of the red widow is found on young palms and palmettoes, with the tangled part in the inner leaves of the plant, and a sheet of silk extending out over the open, older leaves. Its venom is similar to that of the black widows.

Latrodectus bishopi. **Florida range: Marion to Martin counties. Size and when seen similar to southern black widow.**

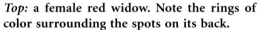

Top: **a female red widow. Note the rings of color surrounding the spots on its back.**

Bottom: **a red widow guarding three eggsacs in its web.**

WIDOW VENOM

Widow venom is an extremely potent neurotoxin (it affects the nervous system) similar to cobra venom, and 15-20 times as potent as rattlesnake venom on an equal volume basis. Widow spider venom causes neurological symptoms such as headache, lightheadedness, and disorientation, also nausea, chills and fever, and especially extreme pain at the site of the bite, with pain migrating to the torso. The abdomen and lower back may become rigid with contractions, a so-called "washboard" effect. In rare cases, convulsions and paralysis of the diaphragm (the muscle by which a person breathes) cause death. Treatment is with antivenin, or in its absence, an injection of calcium gluconate will relieve the symptoms. The only reason widow bites do not result in more fatalities is that the volume of venom is small. Deaths usually occur to people with little resistance to the effects of the venom, i.e., the young, the elderly, and the infirm. Even so, the fatality rate is less than 5% of reported cases.

Recluse Spiders

Family Sicariidae

There are two genera of venomous spiders in this family, *Sicarius* and *Loxosceles*, mostly found in deserts and tropical regions. Only the latter occurs in North America. Two similar species of brown or recluse spiders, *Loxosceles reclusa* and *Loxosceles rufescens*, have been found in Florida from time to time, but not established in the state.

Brown Recluse Spider

The brown recluse is not native to Florida, nor have any widespread established populations been found in the state. It is included because it is occasionally intercepted in the belongings of people who move to Florida. The few known populations in single buildings that the spiders have established so far have been successfully eradicated.

Recluse spiders are tan in color with a brown marking on the head region shaped like a violin. Unlike other spiders similar in appearance, brown recluses only have six eyes (in three pairs) rather than the usual eight. They are not likely to be found outdoors. They prefer dry habitats, which in Florida primarily occur indoors. Here they can hide in and under furniture, in closets, and behind wall hangings. They may venture out at night to hunt for prey. They may then take shelter in clothing or crawl into a bed. Biting of humans occurs when the spider is trapped against the body, otherwise the tiny fangs of this spider would have difficulty penetrating the skin.

The normal attack behavior of a recluse spider is quite stealthy. Prey which trip over the lines of its flimsy web alert the spider, which slowly moves into striking range. Without warning, it lunges forward, nips the victim on a leg, and quickly pulls itself away from the suddenly convulsing prey. The recluse waits for the prey to die, then returns and begins feeding. Perhaps the venom of recluse spiders is so powerful because they normally attack prey that is relatively dangerous to them, like ants and other spiders. A potent venom quickly incapacitates prey while preventing counterattack.

Loxosceles reclusa. **Florida range: scattered reports in North Florida but no established populations evident. Native to the Midwest, and has spread to the Mideast and Atlantic states. Size: Adults of both sexes about 8-10 mm in length.**

Loxosceles rufescens. **Mediterranean brown spider. Similar in all noticeable respects to native brown recluse. Native to southern Europe and northern Africa. Florida range: isolated reports from Orlando and Miami.**

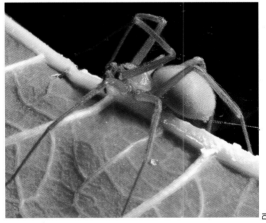

AN UNUSUALLY POWERFUL VENOM

Brown recluse venom is a protein for which no antivenin has been developed commercially because it is so complex. The venom breaks down the connective tissue between cells, which then die. A spreading necrotic (dying tissue), oozing wound develops that depresses into the tissue of the affected region. Severe cases resemble a bullet wound and require skin grafts to heal. Treatment is with antibiotics and corticosteroids. Some success with hyperbaric chambers has been reported as well, although tests have proved inconclusive. One doctor has claimed successful treatment with acupuncture.

Spider Webs

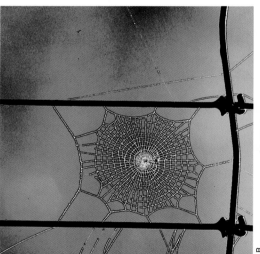

Top: a marsh in early morning gives some idea how numerous spiders can be.

Above, right: this is an open-hub web design.

Above, left: here is a closed-hub web. The orbwebs, with their wagon-wheel shape, represent one of the most basic web designs. Other spider web styles include funnel webs and tangle webs.

Left: the stabilamentum in the web of a young garden spider provides camouflage.

WHY DON'T SPIDERS GET CAUGHT IN THEIR OWN WEBS?

Webs are usually constructed of non-sticky support lines and sticky capture lines. Spiders know where to put their feet to avoid the sticky silk. Also, oil on their feet prevents them from sticking to the capture lines if they accidentally step in the wrong place.

Left: a typical sheetweb consists of a flat or bowl-shaped horizontal sheet, with many isolated cross strands above the sheet which serve as knockdown threads. Small insects which jump or fly into a cross strand are knocked down onto the sheet. The spider waits underneath to bite through the sheet and grab the prey. Often there is a barrier web below the sheet as well, which protects the spider from potential predators.

Above: The silk does not squirt out. The spider uses its feet to pull the silk from the spinnerets.

Above: silk emerging from the spinnerets in multiple strands.

Above: a spider spinning silk for its eggsac. For wrapping purposes the spider can produce many strands at once.

SPIDER SILK

The defining attribute of spiders is the presence of abdominal silk glands and the associated spinnerets which extrude the silk. Spiders (with the exception of pseudoscorpions and some mites) are the only non-insect to make silk, and it is a skill they all have, from the daintiest web spider to the largest giant tarantulas. While tarantulas and many other spiders don't spin webs, all spiders use silk to protect their eggs. Because they use silk to make eggsacs, it seems possible this was its original use by the ancient ancestors of spiders.

Spiders have come a long way since then, and some modern spiders can produce up to seven different types of silk, using different spigots on the spinnerets to produce each type. They can also make the strands thicker or thinner by controlling the width of the spigot's opening.

Spiders use different kinds of silk for different functions, and webs are built of more than one type. A good example is the orbweaving spider which uses dry support silk for the radiating lines and sticky silk for the spiral capture threads.

Silk is a complex protein; it is not the ingredients, but the way the molecules are put together, that makes spider silk special. Amino acids serve as units of structure for proteins. A silk strand is made up of two types of amino acid chains: those in a rigid crystalline structure, and those in a more tangled disorganized structure. It is this composite nature that makes spider silk so strong. Spider silk has the best attributes that both kinds of amino acid chains can offer: strength <u>and</u> stretch.

Spiders don't squirt the silk from their spinnerets (the silk-producing organs) located on the ends of their abdomens, but pull the silk strands using their hind legs.

pulling not only draws the silk out, but it pulls the molecules into the right shape to make the amazingly sturdy silken strands. Until the molecules are lined up in a crystalline structure, the silk is water soluble. After it is stretched it is tough stuff indeed!

Spider silk is the envy of human engineers. There are two main reasons: it is one of the strongest substances, stronger than steel or Kevlar® (used to make bullet-proof vests), and spider silk can stretch up to three time its length. Pretty impressive considering that spiders make silk out of flies and beetles! Not to knock the competition, but insect silk is not nearly as strong as spider silk, even though insect silk is similar in chemical makeup. This is perhaps because insects don't need to use silk to catch prey, but use it to wrap their cocoons or to hang from draglines.

ALL ABOUT SPIDER WEBS

Webs come in many more shapes than the well-known orb web with its "wagon wheel" design. Webs may be broken down into four major categories based on general design: orb, sheet, tangle, and funnel.

Orb Webs: Orb webs are built by several different families of spiders, but all orb webs share the basic design of a central hub, radial lines like wheel spokes extending out from this hub, and a sticky spiral of adhesive silk. Despite its apparent sophistication, orb webs are thought to be more primitive than some of the other web styles because this type of web is used by several families of spider, some of which retain otherwise primitive characteristics.

Many orb weavers that hunt at night take down or eat their webs in the morning, then rebuild them in the evening. This habit protects them from predators that might notice the web in daylight. Some of the orb weavers that make very large webs do not take them down every day, but many of this group abandon the web for a safer hiding place nearby during the day. They may crawl into nearby Spanish moss, a rolled leaf, or small crevice to wait for dark.

A web can be built in about half an hour. A spider sitting at the center of its web can immediately detect where in the web its prey is trapped. Once the spider has located the position of the prey from its waiting spot on the hub, it may pluck at the web to get a better feel of how big the prey is, then run down the radial lines to bite and/or wrap the hapless insect. Often a spider will lay a dragline from the hub for extra security.

Spiders make many kinds of silk. There is the well-known sticky silk and also something called cribellate silk. Cribellate silk is sticky without any adhesive. Cribellate silk can be thought of as similar to fluffy strands of yarn. It works by tangling in the spines and hairs of the insect prey. Spiders which make cribellate silk do it by fluffing the silk coming out of a special set of spinnerets called the cribellum. The fluffing is done with a comb-like structure located on the fourth pair of legs, the calamistrum.

Sheet Webs. Sheet webs lack the wonderful symmetry of orb webs, but they do their job well enough. These webs can be built off the ground in vegetation to catch flying insects as well as on the soil. The sheet web always has one or two silken sheets parallel with the ground. This sheet (or two) is embedded in a matrix of support lines and knock-down threads. These knock-down threads intercept the flight of insects and knock them down onto the sheet for capture by the spider which is waiting beneath. Sheet web weavers in Florida belong to the family Linyphiidae. They use no sticky glue, but rely on web structure alone to hold the prey long enough for the spider to grab it.

Tangle Webs. The tangle web is like a sheet web without the sheet. Mostly just the knockdown threads remain, which are loosely organized in certain areas of the web. Tangle webs do have a basic design, but are highly variable, and still look like a mess when compared to an orb web. Nevertheless, the group of spiders which build tangle webs are very successful and includes the comb-footed spiders.

One advantage tangle web weavers have is that they can put these webs anywhere, whereas orb weavers have to be fairly selective. This is because the web design of a tangle web is so flexible. Tangle webs generally consist of a rough platform with suspending threads hanging from a support at the top, and threads connecting to the ground. These lower threads may be sticky, and ensnare insects trying to walk through them on the soil.

Funnel Webs. The funnel web is a design that combines a hiding place and a hunting site. The narrow end of the funnel web generally extends into a crack in the support where the spider can wait for prey. The funnel extends out into a large sheet. Funnel webs may have knock-down threads or can be sticky, depending on the type of spider that makes the web.

GBE

Opposite page, top: spider webs can be so numerous that they are effectively like flypaper.

Above: the web of a small orb weaver sits above the sheet web of a bowl and doily spider, making a spider condominium.

Right: a spider's meal wrapped in silk and hanging by a line. This garden spider finds grasshoppers to be one of its favorite meals.

Far right: a new web under construction. The spiral of this web is a temporary scaffolding which will help the spider to lay down the sticky spiral. It will be taken up as the sticky spiral is laid down.

DL

DL

Orbweaving Spiders

Family Araneidae

Orbweaving spiders build the typical wheel-shaped web which most people associate with spiders. This is one of the larger groups of spiders in the world. A number of species of orbweavers are found in Florida.

Giant Lichen Orbweaver

The giant green orbweaver is mottled with black, gray, and lichen green colors. It makes a large orb web up to a meter in diameter. The webs are made in moist wooded areas, often near water. It frequently hides during the day. It finds shelter in bark crevices or in Spanish moss.

Araneus bicentenarius. **Florida range: northern half of the state. Size: females 20-25 mm, males 12-14 mm. When seen: late spring to mid-summer.**

Left: **this female giant lichen orbweaver begins the act of web-building by starting a frame thread.**

Center: **the green and black color of this humpbacked orbweaver is perfect camouflage in the lichen growing on oak bark, where it hides during the day.**

Bottom: **the unusual multi-pointed humps of this rare, frilled orbweaver are its most distinctive feature.**

Humpbacked Orbweaver

This small orbweaver is variable in color, often brownish with a foliar (leaf-like) pattern on the abdomen. One color form is mostly lichen green, with the folium black. This color form blends particularly well into lichen-covered bark. The brown form sits on twigs during the day and looks like a bud. Both color forms have a bump (or tubercle, a rounded projection) at the end of the abdomen. This species makes its moderate-sized orbweb in wooded areas at night and takes it down before dawn.

Eustala anastera. **Florida range: statewide. Size: females 5-6 mm in length, males 4-5 mm. When seen: spring to summer.**

Frilled Orbweaver

This small orbweaver makes a very rudimentary web where it hangs at night. It emits a pheromone (sex attractant) that entices small male moths to come within grabbing distance. During the day, the spider looks like just another bud on a twig. The tiny male is rarely seen, but one was found sitting next to this female (see upper left corner of photo).

Kaira alba. **Florida range: statewide. Size: females 6.5-7.3 mm in length, males 2.6-3 mm. When seen: females all year, males in early summer.**

Spotted Orbweavers (right)

There are several species of the genus *Neoscona* in Florida. Two are moderately large spiders which make large orbwebs in autumn. These spiders are named "spotted" because they have two rows of black spots on the back of the abdomen converging toward the rear.

Neoscona domiciliorum. **Florida range: statewide, common in open woodland and woods edge. Size: female 7-16 mm, male 8-9 mm. When seen: autumn. The black, white, and red colors of this species make it distinctive from its close relatives.**

Triangle Orbweaver (above)

This medium-sized orbweaver has a triangular-shaped abdomen, and is found in open woodland. It is an unusual orbweaver in the sense that it hangs in the middle of its web with its head pointed upward. The other species either hang upside down, or with the head pointed downward. Perhaps this posture gives it an advantage in watching for birds that might try to swoop down and snatch it out of its web.

Verrucosa arenata. **Florida range: northern peninsula, Panhandle. Size: female 5-9.5 mm, male 4-6 mm. When seen: late summer to autumn.**

Starbellied Orbweaver (left)

The most common of four species in this genus which occur in Florida, this spider can be found in grassland and open woodland. It is mostly brown, with a radial crown of blunt spines on its abdomen.

Acanthepeira stellata. **Florida range: statewide. Size: female 8-9 mm, male 4-5 mm. Seasons seen: late spring to early autumn.**

Top, right: **this redfemured spotted orbweaver hangs in its web in a typical head down position from where it monitors vibrations in its web.**

Tropical Orbweaver

The tropical orbweavers are surprising because of their jumbo size. They come out at night to spin very large webs across paths and driveways.

The spiders are a dull-brown color, sometimes with white or yellow "shoulders" on their rounded abdomen. Individual females may have abdomens as large as a lady's wristwatch.

A large female can rival the golden silk orbweaver in the size of its ambitious web. These webs can span several yards of space, with the orb almost a yard across. The tropical orbweavers seem to favor forest edges and other open areas to build their webs in the evening. This is why they are usually seen along roads and paths. They sit in the center of their web at night, awaiting large flying insects like moths. During the day they can be found sitting huddled in a curled-up leaf at the end of one of the bridge threads holding up their web.

Juveniles are quite variable in the color of the abdomen. Some have white spots which form a cross on the abdomen. Others are leaf green on the top of the abdomen.

Eriophora ravilla. Florida range: statewide. Size: females 12-24 mm, males 9-13 mm.

Top, left: a female tropical orbweaver sits in a normal resting position. During the day, the spider hides in a rolled leaf.

Top, right: this sub-adult female exhibits an alternate color pattern, seen in males, but not in adult females.

Above: the enlarged palps of this male are used for mating.

Right: juvenile tropical orbweavers are just the right size to be preyed on by mud dauber wasps, which provision their mud nests with paralyzed spiders to feed the larval wasps.

Basilica Spider

The basilica spider spins a horizontal orbweb in the shape of a dome superficially similar to that of the filmy dome spider. This shape gives it its name, a reference to the high, domed ceiling inside some cathedrals. Like the filmy dome spider, the basilica spider places its web in the understory of forests and hardwood hammocks.

Even though the web of the basilica spider is similar in design to those of the filmy dome and the bowl-and-doily spiders, these spiders are not closely related. The basilica spider and its web are larger than the other two dome-builders, and the weave of the web is different. The actual mesh of the dome has a distinctive square pattern to it. It also relies on being sticky to capture insects rather than the tangled snare of the filmy dome and bowl-and-doily spiders.

Mecynogea lemniscata. Florida range: statewide. Size: female 6-9 mm, male 5.0-6.5 mm. When seen: summer and autumn.

Top: a female basilica spider in her normal resting position.
Center: this basilica spider sits among dead twigs. Tops of shrubs are typical places to find this type of web.
Right: a basilica spider places her bluish-gray eggsacs on a string above the top of the dome of her web. So, its not necessary to see the spider to identify a basilica spider web.
Far right: this basilica spider is searching for just the right place to begin building its web.

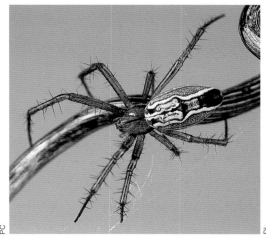

Spiny Orbweavers

This subgroup of the orbweaver family has hard-tipped spines on the abdomen which protects them from predators like birds and lizards. They also have a glossy, enameled look. Florida representatives of this group include the arrowshaped, spiny-crowned, and spinybacked orbweavers. Males are very small and not easily seen, unless they are hanging out around the edge of a female's web. Females lay their eggsacs on tree bark and leaves.

Arrowshaped Orbweaver (right)

This orbweaver has two main spines sticking out the back with two pairs of smaller spines farther forward. It makes a small orb web in shrubbery. Typically, it is yellow, black, and reddish brown in color.

Micrathena sagittata. Florida range: statewide. Size: female 8-9 mm, male 4-5 mm. When seen: summer and autumn.

Spiny Crowned Orbweaver

(far, right)

Similar in size to the arrowshaped orbweaver, this species has more but smaller spines on the abdomen. it is black and white in color, but the proportion of each color can vary considerably.

Microthena gracilis. Florida range: statewide. size: females 7.0-10.8 mm, males 4.2-5.1 mm. When seen: summer.

Top: **the underside of an arrowshaped orbweaver is blotched with yellow.**

Above: **the prominent spines on the end of the arrowshaped orbweaver show how it got its name.**

Right: **a relative of the arrowshaped orbweaver which has even more, but shorter spines, is the spinycrowned orbweaver.**

Spinybacked Orbweaver

Also called the "star" or "jewel box spider," these odd, spiny, little spiders can be common around houses and in hardwood hammocks. There is no mistaking this spider as it has a flattened, white abdomen with red spines around the outside edge. One idea to explain the function of these thorns is that it makes these spiders hard for birds to swallow. Looking at the spines, it is not hard to see how they would make this spider look like more than a mouthful.

The "crab" spider puts little tufts of silk in its web. It seems that these little flags serve a warning function to prevent birds from flying into the web, destroying it.

The attractive egg sac is about 3/4 of an inch (1-2 cm) in length. It is made from yellow silk with a green stripe down the middle of its long axis. It is often placed on the underside of a leaf.

Gasteracantha cancriformis. **Florida range: statewide. Size: females 8-10 mm, males 2-3 mm. When seen: summer and autumn.**

Top: the underside of a spinybacked orbweaver looks quite different than the top side.

Above: a typical female spinybacked orbweaver, with its black, white, and red color.

Left: this specimen exhibits some of the yellow coloration found in the same species in the tropics. For example, in South America, this species is yellow instead of white, and the spines are black instead of red.

Garden Orbweavers

These common, large spiders are found throughout most of the US.

They build their webs in overgrown fields, along field edges and in open woods. They rebuild these webs each morning before they begin their daily wait for prey. Garden orbweavers only become conspicuous to casual observers late in the summer when the very big female matures. The much smaller male can sometimes be spotted in the web, waiting for his chance to mate.

Florida is home to a total of four closely-related species in this genus, more than any other state. They all share large size, yellow, black, and silver coloration, and the habit of placing an area of conspicuous, white, silken banners in their webs called the 'stabilimentum.'

Yellow Garden Orbweaver (right)

Argiope aurantia. Florida range: statewide, abundant. Size: females 14-25 mm, males 5-6 mm. When seen: summer and autumn. The stabilimentum makes a vertical zigzag band above and below the middle. The stabilimentum of small juveniles forms a central circle where the spider sits.

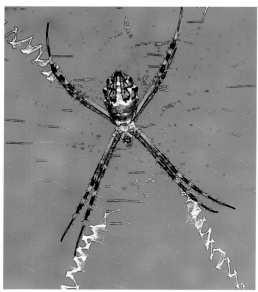

Banded Garden Orbweaver

(opposite page, top)

Argiope trifasciata. Florida range: statewide but not common. Size: females 12-26 mm, males 5-6 mm. When seen: summer and autumn. Stabilimentum similar to *A. aurantia.*

Silver Garden Orbweaver

(opposite page, bottom)

Argiope argentata. Florida range: south of Lake Okeechobee. Size: females 12 mm, males 4 mm. When seen: all year. Four stabilamenta form a cross, often incomplete, connected in the middle by the spider.

Above, left, and above: the two stabilimenta shown here are those of juveniles of different ages. The one above is a very young, the one shown above left is a little older.

Left: a cross-shaped stabilimentum is the mark of some adult garden spiders, in this case, a Florida garden spider. The silver garden spider makes a similar web.

Opposite page, top and bottom: notice how these two spiders have bunched their eight legs in pairs of two so that it appears from a distance that there are only four legs. This is a common spider behavior. The four leg pairs blend into the four parts of the stabilamentum, camouflaging the spider.

THE STABILIMENTUM

The stabilimentum has generated a surprising amount of debate among spider biologists, perhaps because it is so conspicuous and yet serves no clear function. A fair amount of research effort has gone into determining its usefulness. There are four contending schools of thought about how these bright, white banners might benefit the spider.

First, the name, stabilimentum, implies that it stabilizes or strengthens the web.

Second, it may serve to keep birds from flying into the web by making the web more obvious. A bird accidentally flying through the web would destroy it. This would do the spider no good, and no bird would enjoy finding itself covered in sticky silk!

Third, because the banners reflect ultraviolet light, they may serve to attract flying insect prey, such as bees, that look for the ultraviolet light reflected off of flowers when searching for food.

Fourth, perhaps the spider actually uses the stabilimentum as camouflage to make itself less conspicuous to predators while hanging in the web. Recent research seems to suggest that this last hypothesis is correct, but perhaps some of the other possibilities are valid too.

Longjawed Orbweavers

Family Tetragnathidae

Members of this family of orbweaving spiders often have a distinctly long body. Both sexes (especially males) of some genera have especially long jaws, hence the family common name. Most species build an orb web oriented horizontally or at an angle. The genus *Tetragnatha* in particular is known for making its webs in the vegetation along creeks and lake shores.

Green Longjawed Orbweaver

This longjawed orbweaver is another nocturnal web spider. The female is recognized by its long, slender body, marked with green and silver stripes. Males are almost entirely green.

These inconspicuous little spiders are related to the much larger golden silk spider and share their elongated body shape. They get their name from their elongated jaws, or chelicerae. This small orbweaver can be found in pine needles and Spanish moss

Tetragnatha viridis. Florida range: northern half of state. Size: female 5.7-7.4 mm, male 4.4-6.7 mm. When seen: spring to summer.

BOOKLUNGS

This primitive breathing apparatus is like a stack of papers or the pages of a book. Some might say it more closely resembles the floors of an open parking garage since there are spaces between each sheet through which air circulates. Oxygen diffuses through the walls of the lung chamber and into the spider's blood. There is no pumping action.

The primitive spiders have two booklungs whereas the more modern spiders have a booklung plus a trachael breathing system, like that of insects, in which tubes send oxygen directly to various parts of the body.

PC

DL

SPIDER HABITATS

Because each spider species has certain needs, and has to meet these needs to stay alive, only certain spiders are found in specific habitats. For instance, longjawed orbweaving spiders like it wet, and burrowing wolf spiders like it dry. This is why longjawed orbweavers are found in the cattails along pond edges, and burrowing wolf spiders in open, sandy areas. Each one would not live for very long in the other's habitat. Yes, most spiders are surprisingly choosy! Most people would be too if they had to take their environment exactly as they found it, instead of using climate control.

Top: this female green longjawed orbweaver is quite inconspicuous among the strands of Spanish moss.

Left: a male long-jawed orbweaver mates with its two enlarged palpi. It locks itself in place by grasping the female's fangs beween its own fangs and a large spine at the end of the basal jaw segment on each side.

BK

Orchard Orbweaver (top)

This orbweaver spins its orbweb at an angle and hangs in the center. This spider is a particularly attractive orbweaver with iridescent pink or orange spots on the abdomen which shine like little lights in the dim light of the forest. Why it has these decorations is anybody's guess. It has a slightly elongated abdomen with pale yellow, green, black, and silver markings. It can be very common in woods and hardwood hammocks, often forming groups which attach their webs to each other in areas where there is a lot of food.

Leucauge venusta. **Florida range: statewide. Size: female 5.5-7.5 mm, male 3.5-4.0 mm. When seen: summer and autumn.**

Pale Longjawed Orbweaver
(right)

This yellowish-silver spider is a little larger than the green longjawed orbweaver. It is found in open woodlands and old fields, frequently near streams.

Tetragnatha pallescens. **Florida range: statewide. Size: female 7.3-12.2 mm, male 6.5-9.6 mm. When seen: spring to summer.**

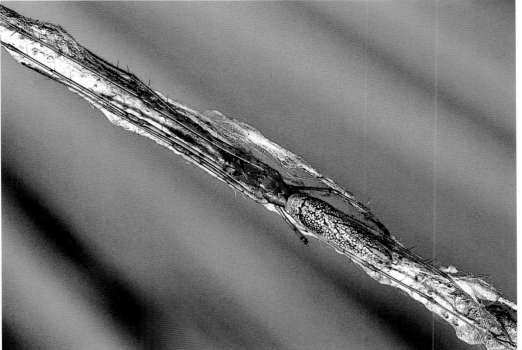

BK

Top: **a typical orchard orbweaver pose as it waits for prey.**

Above: **this longjawed orbweaver remains hidden during the day by stretching out on a twig. The two front pair of legs point forward, the two hind pairs point backward. It makes its small orbweb at night.**

SUCKING STOMACHS

Spider stomachs expand and contract to pump liquid food from the mouth. Solid particles are filtered out. Since spiders have tiny mouths, all chewing is done outside the body by the crushing motion of the fangs and endites.

PC

Golden Silk Orbweaver
(also called the "banana spider")

The golden silk orbweaver is one of the most conspicuous spiders in Florida due to its large size and very big web. It has a long, cylindrical abdomen that can be orange or a greenish-gold color. It is this body shape and color which gives the "banana spider" one of its common names. It also has tufts of black bristles at the joints of three of its four pairs of legs.

It spins a vertical orbweb which can be a meter across. Often the silk has a yellowish color, hence the "golden silk" common name. The golden silk orbweaver sits at the hub of its web waiting for prey. In places where these spiders get a lot to eat, they can grow to be very large. A barrier web, a tangle of silk parallel to the orb, is made on one or both sides to protect the spider from other predators.

Like most web spiders, the male is much smaller than the female, and can be found sitting in the female's web. Often, more than one male can be found in attendance, and they fight among themselves for first access to the female when she matures and is ready to mate. Sometimes the males are missing legs from their fights.

The female banana spider lays her eggs on the sides of trees or under the eaves of buildings near her web. These egg masses are covered in yellowish silk.

Nephila clavipes. Florida range: statewide. Size: females 25-50 mm, males 5-8 mm. When seen: summer and autumn.

PC

Top, right: this view of the golden silk orbweaver shows the golden yellow body color that is very common and is the source of the name "banana spider." Also clear in these photos are the tufts of black hair at the leg joints. The purpose of these hairs is unknown. These spiders are extremely common in the Florida woods. Hikers frequently walk into their huge webs which may be stretched across trails.

Also visible in this photo is a small, male golden silk orbweaver approaching the much larger female in hopes of mating.

Top, left: this view shows the range of body color of golden silk orbweavers. In this photo the spider is more brownish orange and lacks the yellow banana color.

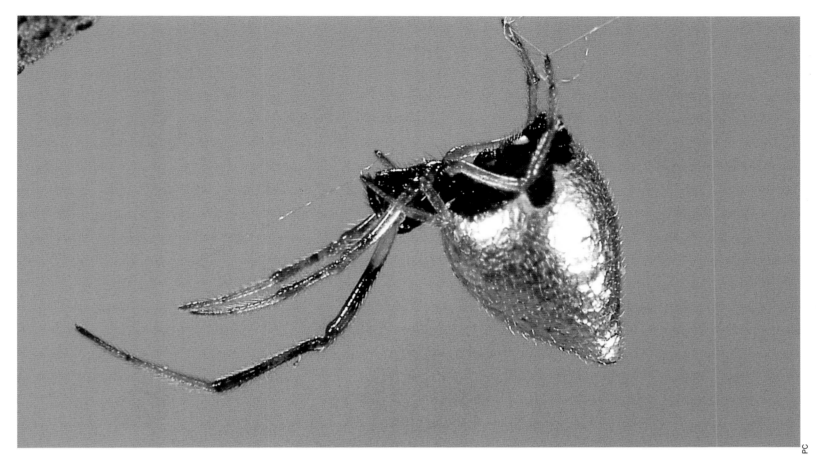

Top: this gorgeous silvery spider (*Argyrodes nephilae*) is a specialized cobweb weaver called a kleptoparasite (literally, a parsitic thief). It lives in the webs of golden silk orbweavers, as well as the webs of a number of other large web weavers. This species enjoys the very great advantage of not having to produce or maintain its own web. It actually avoids the main web of the host spider, preferring to hang out on the frame and barrier web strands. Here it waits until wrapped prey is unattended by the host spider. Then it stealthily sneaks up to the prey, dragging a line behind it which is attached to the barrier web line. Once it attaches its own line, it cuts the thread from which the prey hangs. The prey then swings out into the barrier web. If the *Argyrodes* has done its job well, the host spider will never know it was robbed. But if the *Argyrodes nephilae* makes a mistake, the bigger spider will come charging over to reclaim its prize.

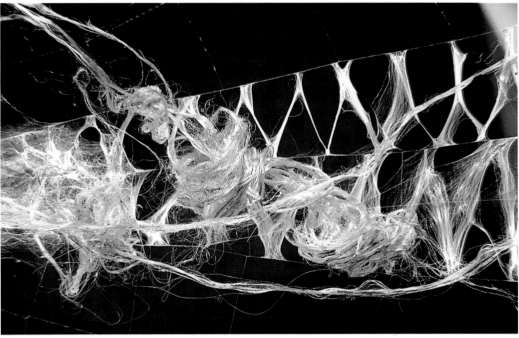

Above: this photo shows the yellow silk produced by the golden silk orbweaver in side-by-side comparison to the whitish silk produced by the yellow garden spider. The difference in color is dramatic.

Right: another view of the golden silk, this time in a web struck by sunlight.

Argyrodes nephila. Florida range: statewide. Size: females 1.7-3.1 mm, males 1.7-2.6 mm. When seen: summer to autumn.

SheetWeb Weavers

Family Linyphiidae

Bowl and Doily Spider *(bottom)*

These little sheet-web weavers can be common in hedges around houses. They build a small, woven, silken bowl, and hang underneath (the doily is a silken platform underneath them). The bowl has a silk superstructure above it to suspend it from the vegetation. It includes vertical threads which knock flying insects out of the air and down into the bowl. As the insect struggles to escape the tangle of threads, the spider pulls it down from below. These spiders do not rely on sticky silk to capture insects, as do orbweavers, but on the structure of the web. As you can see by looking at the web, it is such a confusing tangle of silk lines, any insect hapless enough to fly into it is at the mercy of the spider as is struggles to escape this maze. Sometimes several spiders will make their webs on the same plant, making what appears to be a spider condominium.

Frontinella pyramitela. **Florida range: northern and central parts of the state. Size: female 3.0-4.0 mm, male 3.0-3.3 mm. When seen: summer and autumn.**

Blacktailed Red Sheetweaver

This little, red spider, with a black tip on the end of its abdomen, can be incredibly abundant in yards. If one ventures out early in the morning, hundreds of dew-covered small sheetwebs may be seen in the grass.

Florinda coccinea. **Florida range: statewide. Size: 3 mm. When seen: summer.**

Top: **this small, but brightly colored red and black spider may be quite conspicuous in its small sheet web.**

Bottom, left: **the cottony bowl and doily web is a common summer sight.**

ARACHNOPHOBIA (FEAR OF SPIDERS)

There is an important difference between justifiable caution and unnecessary fear and hatred. It is not unreasonable to give some respect and keep a safe distance from a creature that might bite. It is different to feel overwhelming revulsion when merely confronted with a photo of that same creature.

Arachnophobia, a morbid fear of spiders, is a common affliction that is difficult to explain. This fear is not always associated with general timidity or fear of other animals, such as snakes. It is probably not due to the hairiness of spiders because there are many other hairy animals. Also, spiders are generally too small for their hairiness to be visible without a closer approacher than those afraid of spiders would be likely to tolerate. Some biologists suggest that there is an instinctive fear of poisonous spiders, but arachnophobia is most common in cultures of European origin where there are few poisonous spiders and far from tropical areas where the threat would be realistic. Some cases of this fear may come from a childhood trauma, usually some variation of "My big brother grabbed me and put a big spider down the back of my shirt." Some cases may be the result of a child seeing the terrified reactions of parents or other adults when confronted with spiders. Beyond all this, there is something about spiders that could be interpreted as sinister. It may be due to the peculiar movement of spiders. Spider legs are extended by hydraulics rather than muscular contraction. This causes spider movements to be very slow and fluid, which may seem creepy to some. The fear of spiders may be on the increase as more children grow up in urban environments that have few spiders.

Filmy Dome Spider

This is a woodland relative of the bowl and doily spider. It builds a web similar in design, except that the bowl is inverted into an arching dome. These spiders can be found in the low vegetation of forest understory.

Neriene radiata. Florida range: northern and central parts of the state. Size: female 4.0-6.5 mm, male 3.4-5.3 mm. When seen: summer and autumn.

Right: a female filmy dome spider waits for her prey. Note how many web spiders hang upside down, the better to attack prey from the appropriate direction (its also easier to support their weight this way).

Bottom: a typical woods edge habitat for the filmy dome spider.

FLORIDA HABITATS

It is helpful to have an idea of where to find spiders, and why there are so many different kinds. A particular habitat is the typical place where a plant or animal lives. People make their own habitat, from building houses to turning on the air conditioning. People can travel the length of Florida in an air-conditioned car in a day, but a little 'bug' may spend its whole life under one rock. Why? A little critter like a spider can quickly die of heat or cold or thirst if it is outside its natural habitat. The little bodies take on the temperature of the environment. Because humans have such large bodies, and make their own heat internally, they can tolerate a wider range of temperatures and humidity.

Florida has many different types of habitats. And, for most of them, it is a story of water. Everyone has heard of Florida's famous swamps and beaches, but there are also special places found nowhere else in the world. One of these is the high, dry scrub and sandhill habitat (essentially wet desert) found anywhere there is a sandy ridge. Scrubs and sandhills (distinguished by their plant associations and the type of sand) are found state-wide, except at the southern tip of the peninsula where the ground is rocky.

There are also hardwood hammocks, found in slightly elevated areas more moist than scrubs, but not too wet. In these places live majestic live oaks and the cold-hardy cabbage palm.

Pine flatwoods are all over the state in flat areas which vary in wetness. There are also cypress swamps near flowing freshwater and lakes, and mangroves near the ocean.

Temperature plays a role too. In northern Florida are forests with maple and sweetgum trees, like in more northern US, and in the southern parts of the state are forests with trees more in common with Caribbean islands.

Cobweb Weavers

Family Theridiidae

This is a large family of mostly small spiders which make tangle webs. It includes the widow spiders which are covered in this book in the venomous spider chapter

---

Spotted Yellow Cobweb Weaver

(right)

This spider may be commonly found in overgrown weedy areas.

Theridion pictipes. **Florida range: north of Lake Okeechobee. size: females 2.8-5.0 mm, males 2.5-3.5 mm. When seen: spring.**

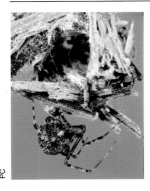

Left: a tent cobweb weaver sits just below the opening to its tent which is made of debris.

Common House Spiders *(above)*

The similar common house spider and the tent cobweb weaver are abundant spiders that can be seen in typical tangled webs under eaves and around windows. The tent cobweb weaver is so named because it makes a cone-like tent from small leaf and twig pieces in the middle of its web where it hides. Males are very tiny.

Tidarren sisyphoides. **Florida range: statewide. Size: females 5.8-8.6 mm; males 1.3-1.4 mm. When seen: spring to summer.**

Social Cobweb Spider *(left)*

Spiders are famous for being cannibalistic and otherwise unfriendly toward their relatives. The social cobweb spider is an exception to this rule. These small spiders live together in the webs of their mother and remain there until just before they are ready to breed themselves. At this point, they each strike out on their own. The females each start their own colonies, and their brothers look for mature females to mate with. While young, they share in web maintenance and prey capture, and even share food. Their webs can be found in the branches of small trees and shrubs near water. It is possible to mistake their webs for tent caterpillar colonies, but a close look will reveal spiders. The colonies are not large. They may be only the size of a grapefruit.

Anelosimus studiosus. **Florida range: statewide. Size: female 3.2-4.7 mm, male 2.1-2.3 mm. When seen: colonies seen year-round.**

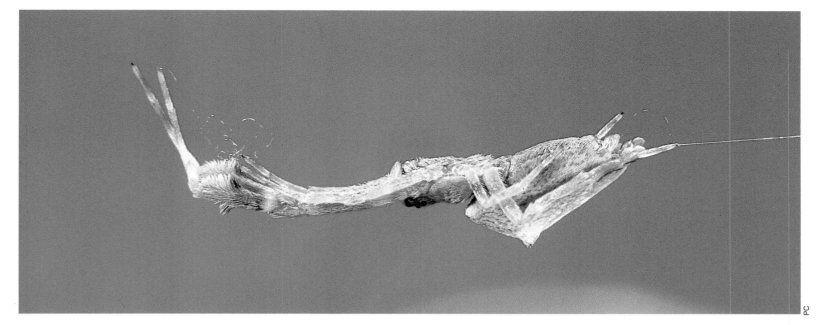

Featherlegged Orbweaver

As its name implies, this species has fringes of hairs on its legs giving it a feathery appearance. It makes a small, horizontal cobweb. Within the web, a female spider will string both its eggsacs and prey remains in a line resembling a twig, where it will sit and hide.

Uluboros glomosus. **Florida range: statewide. size: females 2.8-4.3 mm, males 2.3-3.2 mm. When seen: summer and autumn.**

Top: **this female featherlegged orbweaver is sitting on a frame thread prior to making its web.**

Right: **the hackled silk gives this orb web an unusual appearance, and provides camouflage for the spider, sitting in the middle.**

WEB-SPINNING SPIDERS

A spider's web provides a whole range of advantages to its creator. It greatly inproves the spider's reach, grabbing prey that is moving too far away and too fast for the spider to catch. Once the web is set up, the spider need not endure the rigors of the hunt, but can simply shut down its energy-consuming activities, rest and wait. Prey that get caught in the web are already partly subdued, or at least confused, and pose less of a threat to the spider. The web also functions as a defense, protecting the spider from certain predators, such as dragonflies.

WEBS AND THE AMATEUR NATURALIST

For those interested in discovering the secrets of nature, spider webs present many interesting questions. A person can walk into a Florida state park or even a back yard and find much to study. What is the function of the dome of the filmy dome spider? Why does the spinyback orbweaver place tufts of silk around the edges of its web? Why is the orb web of the orchard orbweaver at an angle instead of vertical like that of most other orbweavers? Why does the southern crevice spider make such a conspicuous web? What are the engineering features that dictate the structure of the apparently chaotic "tangle webs" of species such as the black widow and the common house spider? The answers to these questions would reveal something meaningful about how these spiders make a living.

THE WISDOM OF THE WEB

For thousands of years, people saw the precisely engineered webs of spiders as proof that even the smallest animals were intelligent. Early observers realized that each kind of spider made only one kind of web, but this was not immediately recognized as an example of unthinking behavior. Instead, it appeared to show that each spider knew its place in the world and remained within its hereditary profession. This idea has always appealed to those seeking to defend traditional ideas about class and caste among humans. The argument was that such social arrangements are merely an extension of natural law. This concept of the world was finally debunked as behavioral sciences showed that a spider spinning its web was very different from a fisherman knotting his net. The gap between the rational abilities of humans and the instinctual patterns that control the behavior of many other creatures, especially spiders and insects, was shown to be very large.

Spiders That Throw Nets

Bolas Spider

The bolas spider is related to the orbweaving spiders, but has evolved an amazing behavior for prey capture. Its common name is a clue to its unique method. The word 'bolas' refers to a type of lasso used by the Gauchos of the Argentine pampas. The Argentine bolas consists of three ropes joined at one end, and with weights on opposite ends. When thrown at a running steer, the whirling ropes entangle the animal's legs. While the spider does not throw a lasso, it does swing a strand of silk with a droplet of adhesive glue at the end.

In the evolutionary process, the bolas spider has dispensed with its web, and captures prey by enticing it within striking distance using a scent as a lure. The spider gives off a chemical that mimics the sex pheromone of a female moth. The spider thus fools male moths into flying toward the lure. Then the spider swings the sticky bolas, hits the moth, and reels him in.

Mastophora spp. Florida range: northern and central parts of the state. Size: female 14 mm, male 2 mm. When seen: summer and autumn.

Top: a male moth flies upwind, following in the dark the simulated (and fraudulent) scent of a prospective mate released by the bolas spider. The bolas spider, hanging by a silk thread, has prepared a gob of sticky silk (the bolas) and cocked its leg in anticipation of flicking it at the moth. This spectacular and unique photograph is by Florida scientist Mark Stowe, and was taken at the Devil's Millhopper, a large sinkhole near Gainesville.

Left: this photo, taken seconds after the one at the top of the page, shows that the spider has made a successful strike and the moth prey is now helplessly tethered.

Bottom, right: bolas spiders often sit on a branch during the day where they look like a bud. When sitting on a leaf they look like a bird dropping. Either way, they are well camouflaged.

Ogrefaced Spider

Family Deinopidae

The ogrefaced spider is easily one of the most interesting spiders in the US. It hunts by casting a small web, held like a fisherman's cast-net in its front legs. The net captures prey walking on the ground, crawling down a branch, or flitting through the air.

The ogreface spider gets its name from its large, forward-facing eyes, and is among the animals with the best night vision. All the better to see its prey! It hunts at night, while hanging from a silk scaffold. It makes the little capture net of cribellate silk that adheres to prey by being fluffy like yarn rather than by being sticky. The spider hangs head-down until a small insect walks underneath; then it slaps the web down over the insect and pull it up, all entangled.

Oddly, the eyes of the ogreface spider are so specialized for night vision, that it is virtual blind during the day. It hides by stretching out along a twig.

Deinopis spinosa. Florida range: statewide. Size: female 20 mm, male 15 mm. When seen: summer and autumn.

Top: the ogrefaced spider deploys it net, ready for action.

Above: the two large eyes of the ogrefaced spider which give it its name.

Right: the ogrefaced spider camouflages itself during the day by blending with a branch.

BM

Funnelweb Spiders

Family Agelenidae

Sometimes also called grass spiders, these striped, gray spiders look a bit like narrow wolf spiders with long spinnerets. Their eye arrangement is unremarkable, however.

These spiders are much more common farther north, where they can be abundant in hedges and fields. In Florida, they tend to occur in drier habitats, and there are only a few species.

Agelenopsis sp. Florida range: statewide. Size: both sexes 10-15 mm. When seen: summer to autumn.

Top: a funnelweb spider waits for prey to fall on its web.

Right: a male funnelweb spider finds a female's web and begins searching for her.

PC

Rosemary Wolf Spider

The rosemary wolf spider has one of the most restricted ranges known for any spider. It is only found in a 3,000 acre scrub habitat of Putnam County. It is named after Florida rosemary, a shrub typical of Florida's scrub habitats. Like many scrub organisms, the rosemary wolf spider is threatened by development of its habitats for housing and orange groves. Because its entire distribution is in one small area, it is considered endangered. In general appearance, it is much like the field wolf spider.

Lycosa ericeticola **Florida range: scrub habitats of Putnam county. Size: 25.0 mm. When seen: spring to autumn.**

FISHING WITH WEBS

The natives of New Guinea make use of strong spider webs found in the forest. These webs can be up to six feet in diameter. The natives set bamboo poles in the ground which at the top are bent into a large hoop. In a short while, spiders use the frame to weave a web, which is then used (usually only once) as a fishing net to snare fish in a stream. An alternative method is to use the bamboo hoop to scoop up the webs of several spiders, thus producing an even stronger net.

SPIDER HUNTING WASPS

Spiders are armed in front with insect-stopping toxins, from the rear issues entangling silk, and the long legs confer a wrestler's reach. Spiders do not seem easy victims. Nevertheless, there are many species of wasps in Florida that are professional spider hunters. Most impressive of these are the spider wasps of the family Pompilidae, most of which are long-legged and dark-colored, sometimes with a red band on the abdomen. These wasps can often be seen racing over the ground in their never-ending quest for spiders; as they run, they have the peculiar habit of flicking their black wings open and shut. The goal of these wasps is to find a spider, paralyze it with a sting to the nerve center on the underside of the body, drag it off to a secure location (usually an underground burrow) and lay an egg on it. The larval wasp is given only one spider, so the mother wasp is forced to challenge a spider her own size or larger if she is to produce offspring her own size. The contest between wasp and spider is a flurry of movement too fast for the eye to follow as the wasp zips around the spider, which is frantically attempting to defend itself.

Box photo: another wasp tactic---a parasitic wasp laying its egg directly into the eggsac of a yellow garden orbweaver. The baby spiders will become food for the baby wasp.

PC

Trapdoor Spiders

Families Ctenizidae and Cyrtaucheniidae

Trapdoor spiders are widespread in the southern US, and can be very common locally, but are seldom seen due to their secretive lifestyle. They live their lives in silk-lined burrows which they cap off with a hinged door made of silk, soil, and bits of leaves. It is almost impossible to see this door when it is closed.

The only clue that these ancient spiders are in an area may be the appearance of wandering mature males in their season. They are looking for the burrows of sexually-mature females. As these spiders are all but blind, they probably locate the females' burrows by scent.

Trapdoor spiders are very bulky looking (for a spider) and are usually a shiny reddish-brown to black color. While they have big fangs, they are not known to have very strong venom.

Trapdoor spiders are moderately large; females may exceed an inch in body length. These spiders have burrows which vary from a few inches to a couple of feet in length, depending on the species. Shorter burrows are made by the genera *Cyclocosmia* and *Ummidia*, whereas *Myrmekiaphila* can make longer burrows which make them difficult to dig out. Although typically thought to live in rather moist soil, like clay banks of ravines, the latter two genera have been found in very well-drained, sandy soil as well.

BM

Sculptured Trapdoor Spider

Cyclocosmia is one of the most bizarre spiders in Florida. The back end of its abdomen is flattened and ridged in a pattern which looks like an Aztec sundial! This hard rear end is actually used to defend against spider wasps which use this spider as food for their babies. They have a type of trap door in their burrows like spiders of the genus *Ummidia*, but also back this defense up with their ability to block their eight-inch-deep burrow near the bottom where it narrows using their cork-shaped abdomens in case a wasp gets through the trapdoor. This makes it very difficult for the wasp to successfully continue its attack.

This genus is interesting not just because it has an odd-shaped body, but because it is only found in the southeastern US,

Top: a *Umidia* male wanders in search of a female.

Above: *Cyclocosmia torreya,* the Torreya trapdoor spider, emerging from its burrow. Note the highly camouflaged flap which covers the burrow opening, making it almost invisible.

eastern Mexico, and southern China. This scattered distribution is taken as evidence that what we see now is a remnant of a once much more widespread distribution pattern. In Florida, these spiders are protected at Torreya State Park which is west of Tallahassee.

Cyclocosmia torreya. **Florida range: northern Panhandle. Size: female 33 mm, male 18 mm. When seen: females all year, males in winter.**

Other Trapdoor Spiders

Ummidia uses a different strategy. It makes a very thick trapdoor, but unlike *Cyclocosmia*, it has no other protection. If a wasp tries to enter, the spider hangs on to the corky door for dear life, preventing the wasp from getting in. If the wasp manages to chew through the door or otherwise get in, the poor spider is doomed.

Ummidia spp. Florida range: statewide. Size: 20-50 mm. When seen: females all year, males in winter or summer, depending upon the species.

Myrmekiaphila has yet another strategy. It has a thin door, so a persistent wasp can quickly chew through it. If this happens, the spider runs down its long burrow into a secret branch that also has a trapdoor, hoping the wasp will not notice the burrow is branched. This trick may not always work, but it seems to have helped this species survive.

Myrmekiaphila spp. Florida range: northern half of state. Size: 10-30 mm. When seen: females all year, males in winter.

Top: a view of the Torreya trapdoor spider which shows the unique flattened and ridged rear end of this species which is used to block the burrow as a defense against wasp predators.

Tarantulas

Family Theraphosidae

There are no tarantulas native to Florida, but many species are present in the personal collections of Floridians due to their popularity in the pet trade. This has resulted in the establishment of one species, the Mexican red-rump tarantula (*Brachypelma vagans*), in St. Lucie County. This moderately large tarantula may have a body length up to three inches, and a leg span about twice that. It lives in burrows about 18" deep and about the diameter of a golf ball, in the banks of canals and in the bare ground of citrus groves, usually under the tree canopy.

Brachypelma vagans. Florida range: St. Lucie County. Size: up to 3 inches. When seen: females can be found all year, males in the autumn.

Above, left: the Mexican redknee tarantula, *Brachypelma smithi,* is a species which is a favorite in the pet trade.

Above, right: The Mexican redrump tarantula, *Brachypelma vagans,* has become naturalized in Florida.

EXTERNAL DIGESTION

Spiders use their jaws to break up or at least punch holes in their prey. They then pour in digestive enzymes and suck up the liquid produced as the enzymes digest the prey's internal organs. Spiders cannot swallow chunks of their prey because swallowing is prevented by hair-like filters in the mouth and throat.

Purseweb Spiders

Family Atypidae

Two species of the genus *Sphodros* are found in Florida. Both make a tube-like web that begins a few inches underground, then goes up the side of a tree a foot or more. Essentially, it is a burrow, most of it above ground. Adult webs are half an inch or so in diameter. The webs are covered with bits of sand, bark, moss, and lichen. They look like a piece of root or vine at the base of the tree. Hardwood trees are used almost exclusively, perhaps because this type of tree is predominant in the moist sandy loam soil these spiders prefer. In areas where pursewebs are common, there may be several tubes on each tree.

The most unusual behavior of the pursewebs is their ability to catch prey by impaling it from inside the tube with their extremely long fangs. They hunt by waiting for an insect to walk over the surface of the tube. Once the prey is located, the spider bites right through the camouflaged web. The prey never knows what has hit it and never has a chance to defend itself. Once the spider's venom paralyzes the prey, the spider holds it with one fang, while the other fang cuts a slit in the web and pulls the prey inside. The slit is then mended with silk, and the spider proceeds with its meal.

Although the females of both species are an inconspicuous brown, the males of both species are quite strikingly colored. In the larger and less common *S. rufipes*, the black male has bright red legs. In the smaller *S. abboti*, the male is also mostly black and has a conspicuous iridescent blue or purple abdomen. Ironically, the coloration of the males of these species is thought to make

Top, left: female Abbot purseweb spider

Top, right: a black and blue male Abbot purseweb spider.

Above: the redlegged purseweb spider, male on the left with the colorful legs, and the duller female on the right.

Opposite page: the web of the redlegged purseweb spider is a tube which looks like a root or a vine.

them look like spider wasps, to fool other predators while the males are searching during the day for females!

Sphodros abboti. Florida range: northern half of state. Size: females 12-15 mm, males 10 mm. When seen: females all year, males in late spring to early summer.

Sphodros rufipes. Florida range: northern half of state. Size: females 20-25 mm; males 15 mm. When seen: females all year, males in late spring to early summer.

SOCIAL SPIDERS

There is a whole range of social styles from the "Lone Ranger" spider that lives in its own web and has no contact with other spiders to spiders that build adjacent webs that share certain structural supports, to those truly communal spiders, usually related, that live together, have communal nurseries, and can subdue larger prey than one individual would be able to handle. In most cases, whether webs are built close to each other or actually joined together, the whole group benefits by having a larger insect trap which allows flying insects less room to maneuver. When a fast-flying insect hits one of the webs, it may bounce off, losing momentum, only to land in a neighboring spider's web.

Daddylonglegs (Harvestman)

ORDER OPILIONES

These long-legged arachnids can be distinguished from spiders because their body is all fused into one main part. In this, they resemble ticks and mites, which some scientists think are their closest relatives. Despite reports that they are extremely venomous but cannot bite because their jaws are too small, in fact these animals do not have venom glands and their jaws are adequate, so there is no truth to this "urban legend."

Family Leiobunidae

This family contains the typical, longlegged species that most people think of as daddylonglegs.

Family Cosmetidae

This group of harvestmen are primarily tropical in distribution. All have relatively shorter legs and larger bodies than what Floridians are used to seeing in Daddylonglegs. Generally, they are brightly colored, and often have spines on the back.

Top and above: a *Leiobunum* sp. daddylonglegs may sit in one place for hours. If disturbed, it will start to bounce up and down on its long legs, blurring the outline of its body, and making it difficult for visual predators like birds to get a good look at it. Notice the two eyes on the median hump in the photo above.

Mites And Ticks

ORDER ACARI

The Acari is a very large group of mostly tiny organisms that is even more diverse than spiders. The ones that are mentioned here are among the very few that most people are likely to encounter.

*Top, **left:*** a hitchhiking mite has latched onto the underside of a butterfly.

*Top, **right:*** this crane fly is so loaded down with mites on its head and thorax, it is a wonder that it can even fly.

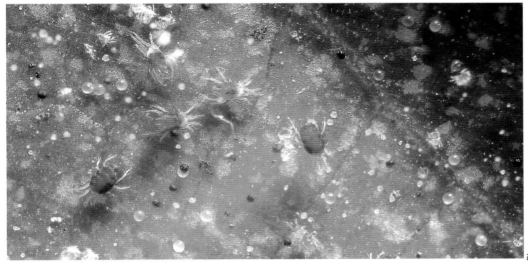

Spider Mites

Family Tetranychidae

These tiny mites spin silken threads all over the leaves they are attacking, hence the name. When large numbers build up, they can kill ornamental plants.

Two-spotted spider mite. *Tetranychus* sp. Florida range: statewide. Size: about 1 mm. When seen: all year, more prevalent in warm weather.

MITES AND TICKS

The mites are a huge group, undoubtedly including hundreds of thousands of species, only a small fraction of which have been described and given names. Most species are microscopic, and many have fantastically specialized habitats. There are, for example, parasitic mites that live only in the lungs of certain snakes, and there are specialized mites that can only be found crawling around on the bodies of one rare species of millipede restricted to patches of Florida scrub habitat on the Lake Wales Ridge. All Florida birds and mammals have their own mites, most of which do no noticeable harm to their hosts. Humans have hair follicle

mites, especially in the eyebrows. These are microscopic and cause no symptoms; for all we know they might be beneficial in some obscure way. Many Florida plants, such as wild grape, have little pockets in their leaves (look at a grape leaf where all the veins meet on the underside near the base). These pockets are apparently adaptations for housing predatory mites that attack other mites that suck sap from the leaves. There are aquatic mites, including some large red species that can be seen swimming near the bottom in the shallows of clear Florida lakes. Adult aquatic insects such as mosquitoes and damselflies are often seen providing

involutary transport for the bright red young of water mites. There is a whole world of mites that completely escapes human notice, except for the small proportion that cause problems, such as the ear mites of cats and dogs, dust mites that may cause allergies, greenhouse mites on cultivated plants, and chiggers. Many mites are covered with peculiar armor-like plates, or patterned with spoon-shaped scales, or provided with precisely arranged sets of long, curling hairs. Ticks are among the giants of the mite world, and provide a glimpse of some of the kinds of specializations found in parasitic mites.

Ticks can carry serious diseases. A potentially fatal disease carried by some Florida ticks is human ehrlichiosis, a disease with flu-like sytems. About 2.5% of the people who contract this disease die. Preventing disease from ticks is a three-step process. First, repellent should be used on clothing to keep ticks off when in the woods. Second, ticks that embed should be removed promptly with tweezers. Third, if someone becomes ill shortly after a visit to the woods, they should seek medical assistance. Lyme Disease is a debilitating disease carried by deer ticks, a species that exists from New England into Florida. Within Florida, however, cases are currently rare. In fact, many entomologists wrongly believe there is no Lyme Disease in Florida. Symptoms for Lyme Disease are not uniform. Some patients develop a red bullseye at the site of the infectious bite. Other individuals do not. Lyme Disease is rarely fatal, but can be debilitating if not treated in time.

Ticks

Family Ixodidae

Ticks are one type of giant mite. Ticks are widely recognized and reviled, and justly so. They are parasites with a barbed bite which makes them difficult to remove. The saliva injected by the bite leaves an itchy place that may take weeks to heal.

Many are vectors of serious disease organisms, transmitting such diseases as Rocky Mountain Spotted Fever, and Lyme's Disease. From time to time, Rocky Mounted Spotted Fever does occur in Florida, but Lyme disease is rare so far. Ticks also transmit a number of flu-like diseases, such as erlichiosis.

In the spring, baby ticks, known as "seed ticks," can be very abundant. Walk into the wrong place, and you can be covered head to toe with dozens of the little bloodsuckers!

Top: eastern blacklegged ticks, also known as deer ticks or wood ticks. The tick on the right is fully engorged with blood.

Above: a size comparison of a young tick with the head of an ordinary straight pin.

Chiggers ("Red bugs")

Family Trombiculidae

Chiggers are an especially troublesome kind of mite. Anyone who has not had chiggers has not been outdoors in Florida during the summer! All it takes is a walk in some wet grass, and the next thing you know, little itchy red spots appear on the ankles, around the waist, and in other unfortunate places where clothing is tight. The juvenile stage of these mites is the culprit, and they are almost invisible. Their bite leaves behind saliva which itches for several days. Adult chiggers, which are large enough to see and are red, are predators of other small creatures and do not bite people. It is a prevalent myth that the chigger larva buries itself inside a bite.

Florida Range: statewide. Size: Juveniles are less than one mm (adults about one mm). When seen: they can't really be seen, but they are prevalent in summer.

Right, above: an adult chigger

Right, below: chigger bites on human flesh are very itchy. However, the chigger is not buried inside the skin as is commonly believed.

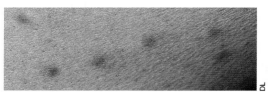

Scorpions

ORDER SCORPIONES,
Family Buthidae

There are few "bugs" as infamous as scorpions. They are immediately recognizable to anyone, from their pincers in front to the stinger on the end of their tail.

Despite their bad reputation, very few scorpions are actually dangerous to humans. While it would certainly not be fun to be stung, none of the species in the eastern US represent a real threat to life and limb.

Scorpions are interesting as they are part of an ancient group of creatures. They have remained virtually unchanged for hundreds of millions of years, and one of the first animals to leave the oceans for the land was a scorpion ancestor! Scorpions looked much as they do now even before insects evolved the ability to fly or spiders the ability to spin webs. Needless to say, they also watched the dinosaurs come and go! So, out of respect for our elders, upon finding a scorpion in the house, perhaps we should consider scooping it up in a dust pan and throwing it out in the back yard away from the house rather than just squashing it flat!

Scorpions in general are secretive creatures, and may only emerge from hiding places at night to forage for smaller creatures. Scorpions are the only arachnid to bear a venomous sting on the last segment of their body. This sting is used for subduing prey as well as for defense.

Scorpions mate by engaging in a face-to-face dance, clasping mouth parts, as the male deposits on the ground a packet of sperm, called a spermatophore, and guides

the female over it so she can pick it up in her genital opening. Scorpions have live birth, with the new-born riding on the mother's back until they shed and disperse.

One of the more interesting facts about scorpions is that they fluoresce (usually green, sometimes blue) when exposed to ultraviolet light. No one knows the purpose of this fluorescence.

THE DANCE OF THE SCORPIONS

Scorpion reproduction is accomplished through a unique mating dance in which the male and female grasp each others pincers and dance back and forth. This dance accomplishes several things. First, by holding each others pincers, there is a safety factor reducing the chance of a predatory response between them. Second, the mating dance serves to clear the area of debris. The male drops a packet of his sperm on the ground in the cleared area and pulls the female toward him. The sperm packet has numerous hooks and when the female's genital opening is directly above the packet, the hooks connect with the female and the packet is pulled toward her body. Thus, she is inseminated and goes off to lay her eggs.

Hentz Striped Scorpion

These scorpions live under stones or piles of refuse, and are also known to climb dead trees, where they can be found resting under loose tree bark. The feed on small insects, including termites. Thankfully, this species does not have very powerful venom and its sting is relatively mild.

Centruroides hentzi. **Florida range: statewide. Size: 32-44 mm. When seen: year-round.**

Florida Bark Scorpion

This large, chocolate brown scorpion is impressive looking but non-threatening to people. While its sting would certainly be painful, it is not known to be dangerous to the average, healthy adult.

Bark scorpions are not as widely distributed as the Hentz striped scorpion. Like that scorpion, they live under tree bark, logs, and trash in places where they can stay moist.

Centruroides gracilis. **Florida range: southern half of the Florida peninsula plus the Keys. Size: 70-110 mm. When seen: year-round.**

Top: a Hentz striped bark scorpion on pine bark, a normal habitat for this species. It is easy to get stung by this species while handling firewood, so gloves should always be worn when bringing firewood inside.

Bottom: a slender brown scorpion, *Centruroides gracilis,* has recently given birth. The babies will ride on her back for several days.

Windscorpions, Camel Spiders

ORDER SOLIFUGAE,
Family Ammotrechidae

Windscorpions, or camel spiders, are common throughout the western US in desert areas, but in the eastern US, are only found in Florida.

These arachnids are among the most primitive of a decidedly ancient group, and there are several distinctive differences between them and the other non-spider arachnids. They have no tail (or venom apparatus) of any kind. They rest in burrows, and come out to hunt insects and other small creatures on the ground. They move very, very fast for an arachnid. Their first pair of legs are modified into feelers and used for grabbing food. They pull the hapless 'bugs' they eat into their fearsome mouth parts, which operate like scissors, cutting the prey into pieces, and passing it into their mouth.

Windscorpions mate face to face, with the male passing a packet of sperm directly

to the female. The female lays a clutch of eggs in a burrow. There is no maternal care.

Ammotrechella stimpsoni. Florida Range: peninsula, Keys. Size: 12-22 mm. When seen: year-round in warm weather.

Top: a windscorpion poses for the camera. Note the large jaws to the right of the eyes.

Below: the face of a whipspider. The large structures in front are the spiny palpi, with which it grabs its prey.

Whipspiders, Tailless Whipscorpions

ORDER AMBLYPYGI,
Family Phrynidae

These unusual looking arachnids live under the bark of dead fallen logs, and under debris in the woods. They are well designed for a two-dimensional existence under bark and logs because they are very flat and move with a side-ways step. They feel around with their very long first pair of legs which function as feelers. They sit and wait for smaller 'bugs' to come within reach, slowly sidle up to them, and then grab them in their fearsome-looking palpi and begin feeding.

Despite their ghastly appearance, tailless whip scorpions lack venom glands and are absolutely harmless to anything bigger than themselves.

The female lays eggs which she carries in a pouch under her body until they hatch.

At this point the young scramble up onto her back where they ride around until they molt and go on their own.

These tiny monsters hide under the bark of damp, rotting logs or even trash, such as piles of wet cardboard. They cannot tolerate dry conditions, so they are almost always found in damp places.

Phrynus marginemaculatus. Florida Range: southern portions of the state. Size: 10.5 - 17 mm. When seen: year-round.

Giant Whipscorpion, Vinegaroon

ORDER UROPYGI,
Family Thelyphonidae

The vinegaroon (also called by the colloquial name "grampus") looks like a big, black scorpion that has lost its tail. Instead of the stinger-bearing tail (or postabdomen) of scorpions, these creatures have a slender antenna-like whip called a flagellum at the end of their bodies. The flagellum serves a sensory function.

The common name (vinegaroon) refers to the smell of their unique chemical defense mechanism. They spray a mixture including acetic acid (the main ingredient of vinegar) from a gland near the base of the flagellum.

The vinegaroons in the US have the distinction of being the largest whipscorpions in the world. Fortunately, these animals, like the whipspiders, lack any venom glands.

Vinagaroons build burrows under logs, rocks, and boards. They hunt by waiting at the entrance at night and wandering around the sand searching for prey. They mate face-to-face like scorpions, with the male

depositing a spermatophore on the ground for the female to pick up in her genital orifice. The female carries her eggs in a pouch under her body, and when they hatch, the young ride around on her back for a period of days. The female may provide mashed prey for the young to feed on before they disperse on their own.

Mastigoproctus giganteus. **Florida Range: peninsula. Size: 38-50 mm. When seen: year-round.**

MS

A FABULOUS WEB

The ladderweb spider (Scoloderus nigriceps) makes its unusual web after dusk. The purpose of the elongated web is to capture moths. A moth is covered with scales which adhere to the web, but come off the moth. This allows it to escape from a normal orbweb. However, if a moth hits the top of a ladderweb, it repeatedly loses scales as it comes loose and falls to a lower part of the web. After it has lost too many scales, the body of the moth sticks to the web, which holds it long enough for the spider to capture it.

SPIDERS ON THE WEB

The American Arachnological Society: http:// americanarachnology.holycross.edu/. This is the premiere arachnological society in the western hemisphere. Professionals and amateurs are welcome to participate. Meetings are held annually.

Arachnology Homepage: http://www. ufsia.ac.be/Arachnology/Arachnology.html. This is primarily a listserver for professional and serious amateur arachnologists. Discussions are intended to be mostly on scientific subjects.

International Society of Arachnology: http://160.111.87.78/ISA/. Like the American Arachnological Society, this newly named society

(previously the Centre International du Documentation Arachnologique) welcomes both professional and amateur members. Meetings are held every 3 years, in widely separate localities around the world.

The American Tarantula Society: http:// www.atshq.org/index.shtml. This website gives information about the activities of the largest tarantula society in the world.

Arachnid Listserver: majordomo@bga.com.